The
NEW
YOU

The NEW YOU

A Guide to Your First 90 Days as a Christian

© 2017 by Robert Hatfield

All rights reserved. No part of this publication may be reproduced, stored in a retrieval system, or transmitted in any form or by any means without the prior written permission of the author. The only exception is brief quotations in printed reviews.

ISBN-13: 978-0-692-92339-9

Published by Sain Publications
PO Box 616 Pulaski, TN 38478
www.sainpublications.com

Printed in the United States of America

Unless otherwise noted, all Scripture quotations are from the New King James Version®. Copyright © 1982 by Thomas Nelson. Used by permission. All rights reserved. Scriptures marked ESV are taken from The Holy Bible, English Standard Version®, copyright © 2001 by Crossway Bibles, a publishing ministry of Good News Publishers. Used by permission. All rights reserved.

Cover Design: Robert Hatfield
Cover Graphic: Shutterstock.com

*To Emily,
who daily exemplifies
the heart of
"the new you."*

CONTENTS

	Preface	9
	Tell Me About Your Baptism	11
	Preliminary Considerations	13
1	The New in You	17
2	A New Goal	27
3	A New Life	37
4	A New Enemy	47
5	A New Standard	57
6	A New Identity	65
7	A New Family	75
8	A New Heart	85
9	A New Home	95
10	A New Job	105
11	A New Mission	115
12	A New Community	125
13	Forever New	133
	Acknowledgments	143

PREFACE

Just before His ascension back to Heaven, the Lord Jesus Christ tasked His apostles with this "Great Commission:"

> 'All authority has been given to Me in heaven and on earth. Go therefore and make disciples of all the nations, baptizing them in the name of the Father and of the Son and of the Holy Spirit, teaching them to observe all things that I have commanded you; and lo, I am with you always, even to the end of the age.' Amen (Mat. 28:18-20).

That charge can be divided into two sections: *first,* Christians are to **GO** preach the gospel to people who do not have a relationship with Jesus (for such is required to "make disciples," Mark 16:15-16). The gospel calls those to whom it is preached to be baptized to be forgiven of their sins (Acts 22:16) and to become children of God (Gal. 3:26-27). *Second,* those new Christians are to **GROW** in their relationship with the Lord. In order for that to be accomplished, someone must teach them "to observe all things that [Jesus] commanded."

This book has been written to accomplish the second half of the Great Commission.

How to Use This Book

Some people may study this book as part of a class, while others may study it on their own. Either way, the best results will be achieved only when you spend significant time in individual Bible study, self-examination, and prayer. To aid you in that process, each chapter is divided into six sections.

One Day at a Time: This section will lead you through a daily study and prayer plan for the next ninety days. Simply read the assigned text, answer the questions, and, if you would like to do so, use the prayer starter as a way to connect your prayer life with what you just read in Scripture.

I cannot overstate the importance of developing a daily Bible study routine. Some new Christians struggle to know where to begin. This section of each chapter will help you. Further, it reminds us that living the Christian life is about making one God-pleasing decision now, with the intention of making another one when the next opportunity presents itself. You take it one day at a time.

What's New?: This part of the each chapter will introduce the lesson and direct you to the main text for the chapter. This is where we will look at the Scriptural standard for which the new you must strive.

Becoming New: Having observed the standard of Scripture, we will then turn to observations and applications from the Bible, noting practical ways that we can become who Christ has recreated us to be.

A Closer Look is the part of each lesson in which we closely examine a particular aspect of that chapter. This is designed to deepen your understanding of a given subject.

Bringing it All Together: We will summarize our findings and distill them into practical action items so we can make these passages from God's word a part of our lives.

The ***Action Items*** provide guidance for ways that you can immediately apply each lesson.

There are ***Questions*** at the end of each chapter. They are designed to guide you through critical thinking. I also hope they will facilitate discussion with other people.

The Christian life is the greatest life possible, but getting started can be overwhelming. I am praying that this book will point you in the right direction and that it will help your heart to seek the Lord as His faithful disciple.

Robert Hatfield
April 25, 2017

TELL ME ABOUT YOUR BAPTISM

Congratulations on becoming a Christian! I am very excited to welcome you into God's family. This is the greatest, most life-changing decision that you will ever make. I am thankful that you believe the gospel of Jesus Christ (John 8:24), and that you are willing to evaluate your life and continually turn away from sin (the Bible calls this repentance, Acts 17:30-31). When you made your initial confession of the name of Christ (Romans 10:9-10), you began a lifetime of confessing His name, knowing that, consequently, He will confess knowing you before the Father (Matthew 10:32-33). What a thrill to be washed by the blood of Jesus in baptism (Acts 22:16; Rom. 6:1-4)! Upon your baptism, the Lord added you to His church (Acts 2:47), and your brothers and sisters in Christ were eager to welcome you into God's family. I am rejoicing with you as you begin your Christian journey!

Let's talk about your baptism. Take a couple of minutes to reflect on the moment you were immersed. Be sure to answer each question. Write your answers in this book.

1. When were you baptized? _____

2. Who taught you what you must do to be saved?
   _____

3. How did you feel about your sins *before* you were baptized?
   _____
   _____
   _____

4. How did you feel *after* your baptism?

_____

_____

_____

_____

5. What changed from the day before your baptism to the day after it? How were you different?

_____

_____

_____

_____

I asked you to write your answers in the book because I want you to preserve the thoughts and feelings that surrounded your baptism. Never forget the impact the blood of Jesus has on your soul. That saving blood will continue to cleanse your soul if you will continue to follow Jesus and obey Him (i.e., "walk in the light," 1 John 1:7).

Your baptism changed you. Sure, you looked the same on the outside (though now I'm sure you wear a big smile as you rejoice in your salvation), but you are completely different on the inside. You have embarked on a journey that will span your lifetime and that leads to eternal life in heaven! This is the journey of the new you.

Over the next ninety days, we are going to study about your new life in Christ. My goal is to take the enthusiasm you feel for Jesus today, and to scale it to jump-start your spiritual growth for the rest of your life. You won't know everything by the end of our time together (even the oldest Christian continues to discover deeper truths about our great God), but you will have a good understanding of what God expects of you as a Christian.

Let's get started!

PRELIMINARY CONSIDERATIONS

Before we dive into the first lesson, I want to remind you of four very important truths.

1. The Bible is God's word.
There are scores of people who make it their practice to attack the Bible's importance and relevance to your life. Don't listen to them. The Bible is God's inspired word (2 Tim. 3:16-17). Every single word was given by God to human writers (around 40 of them), who wrote down exactly what the Holy Spirit revealed to them (1 The. 2:13; 2 Pet. 1:20-21).

In addition to the Bible's *claims* of inspiration, the facts *prove* its authenticity as an inspired document. It is a book of books – 66 to be exact. There are 39 books in the Old Testament, and 27 books in the New Testament. Those 40 inspired writers came from a wide variety of backgrounds. They were herdsmen, kings, scribes, butlers, fishermen and physicians. Some were very well educated, while the learning of others was humble. They wrote in three languages (Hebrew, Aramaic, and Greek). Here's the astounding part: all of this resulted in one unified message. This would be impossible from a human perspective, but it is exactly what God did in the Bible! Yes, God's word is truth (John 17:17)!

2. Truth is truth – no matter what.
God's word is always right. It is never right to compromise truth. People may disagree with it, governments may outlaw it, laws may be made which contradict what it teaches (sanctioning things which the Bible condemns or condemning things which the Bible commands), but the Bible is still true (Acts 5:29).

Truth is true regardless of whether someone accepts it. You became a Christian – the new you – because you studied the Bible, believed it, and knew you must obey it. Consequently, "you have purified your [soul] in obeying the truth" (1 Pet. 1:22). You committed your life to following truth. Do not ever abandon the truth of God's word — no matter what!

3. Your relationship with Jesus is more important than any other relationship in your life.

How did you come to know the Lord? I've known people who were taught the gospel by their parents, their siblings, their spouse, a good friend, a coworker, a girlfriend or a boyfriend. Each of these relationships is special, but *none* is greater than the relationship you now have with the Lord. Jesus said,

> He who loves father or mother more than Me is not worthy of Me. And he who loves son or daughter more than Me is not worthy of Me (Mat. 10:37).

The point is, no relationship is to be placed above your relationship with Christ.

Unfortunately, I have known of circumstances where two people have had a falling out that resulted in at least one of them abandoning their faith. Let me illustrate. Let's say Ethan is a Christian and is dating Emma, who is not a Christian. They study the Bible together, and Emma becomes a Christian. Several months later, they break up. Emma feels it would be too awkward to continue to worship where Ethan worships, so she stops attending worship altogether.

Here's the problem with Emma's decision: she is being unfaithful to God by failing to worship (Heb. 10:25). While the situation may be awkward, maybe there is a way to continue worshiping with the same congregation with the goal of being friends with Ethan (after all, they will be in Heaven together). If that is not an option, then perhaps there is another congregation nearby with which she could worship. Whatever the case, Emma needs to find a workable solution because her relationship with

God must continue even if her relationship with the person who taught her about God is less than ideal. Your relationship with Jesus comes first.

4. Nothing and no one can force you to give up.

Only you can sever your relationship with God. God has promised that He will protect you (1 John 4:4; Rom. 8:31-39), and that He will never leave you nor forsake you (Heb. 13:5). Further, the Bible teaches that "the soul who sins shall die" (Ezek. 18:20), meaning that, if you sin, it is no one's fault but your own. Sometimes Christians make poor decisions that result in sin. When they are asked about it, some try to point the finger at someone or something else, as though their actions were somehow justified. Listen, everyone sins (Rom. 3:23), even Christians (1 John 2:1-2). When we find ourselves back in sin, we should not deny it (1 John 1:8, 10). We must not justify it as if it is OK with God (1 John 1:6). Instead, we must *confess* it.

> If we confess our sins, He is faithful and just to forgive us our sins and to cleanse us from all unrighteousness (1 John 1:9).

The word *confess* literally means "to say the same thing as" someone else. When it comes to sin, the Bible teaches that Christians must confess that sin – that is, say the same thing God says about it.

Let's illustrate it. Nathan has only been a Christian for around a month, so he's still learning about how the Lord wants him to behave. Nathan has been cussing for quite a while, and he does not really think much about the words he uses; it's just how he talks (and so do the people he hangs around). One day, as Nathan is doing his daily Bible study, he comes across Ephesians 4:29:

> Let no corrupt word proceed out of your mouth, but what is good for necessary edification, that it may impart grace to the hearers.

As Nathan thinks about that verse, he realizes that some of his language is "corrupt," and those cuss words do not "impart grace" to people.

What should Nathan do? According to 1 John 1:9, he should confess the sin of corrupt speech. In order to do that, Nathan must "say the same thing God says" about cussing; that is, Nathan must realize that the Bible says corrupt speech is sinful. Having acknowledged such, Nathan then must admit that he has been involved in such activity.

Nathan goes to God in prayer (Acts 8:22), and asks God to forgive him. Then, Nathan goes to those around whom he has used bad language. He explains his new understanding of God's expectations for his speech, and apologizes to them for the way he has talked in the past. Nathan also goes before his church family (James 5:16), and asks them for their help and their prayers.

Nathan immediately begins to amend his speech, carefully thinking before he opens his mouth to speak. The Bible calls this repentance.

The point I'm trying to make is this: Christians should own up to their mistakes and sins. When we mess up, it is no one's fault but our own.

You are in control of your eternal destiny. All of the choices you make are yours. You will not always make the right decisions (I don't always, either), but you must never give up on trying to please God.

* * * * *

These four truths will anchor your new life in Christ:
1. The Bible is God's word.
2. Truth is truth – no matter what.
3. Your relationship with Jesus is more important than any other relationship in your life.
4. Nothing and no one can force you to give up.

Chapter 1
THE NEW IN YOU

ONE DAY AT A TIME

Day One – Read 1 Peter 1:17-25

1. With what were you redeemed?

2. How have you purified your soul?

Prayer Starter – Thank God for giving us His word, the Bible.

Day Two – Read 1 John 1:5-10

1. If we say that we have no sin, we _____ _____.

2. If we _____ our sins, He is faithful and just to forgive us our sins.

Prayer Starter – Thank God for allowing you to have a relationship with Him. Pray that He will help you strengthen your relationship with Him and with His people.

Day Three – Read 2 Corinthians 4:16-18

1. What is happening to the "outward man"? What is happening to the "inward man"?

2. What is the difference between the things which are seen and the things which are not seen?

Prayer Starter – Thank God for the hope of (the fact that we can be confident that we are going to) Heaven.

Day Four – Read 2 Corinthians 5:6-11

1. Who will appear before the judgment seat of Christ?

2. For what will each person give account?

Prayer Starter – Thank God for allowing us to have confidence (hope) that we will be with Him when our lives are over.

Day Five – Read 2 Corinthians 5:12-17

1. If anyone is in Christ, he is a _____ _____.

2. All things have become _____.

Prayer Starter – Thank God for adding you into Christ's kingdom, the church.

Day Six – Read Romans 8:35-39

1. What can separate us from the love of God?

2. In all these things we are more than _____ through Him who loved us.

Prayer Starter – Thank God for victory over life's trials and difficulties. Pray for someone you know who is going through difficulties.

Day Seven – Read 1 Corinthians 6:15-20

1. To whom do we belong?

2. Since we were bought at a price, what are we to do?

Prayer Starter – Pray that God is pleased with your life. Ask Him to open doors through which you can glorify Him. *(To "glorify God" means to honor Him in your actions.)*

WHAT'S NEW?

What's so new about "the new you"? This book is dedicated to answering that question. I want to begin, though, by pointing out that there *is* something new in you!

Paul realized the blessing of being new. Before he became a Christian, Paul (then known as Saul) was convinced that Christianity must be stopped. He was actively involved in murdering and persecuting Christians (Acts 7:54-8:1; 9:1-2). Paul's actions against Christians stemmed from the fact that he didn't believe Jesus is the Lord. All of that changed when the Lord appeared to him while he was traveling to Damascus (Acts 9:3-9). Saul was taught the gospel (by Ananias, who was commanded by the Lord to teach Saul), and he was baptized for the remission of his sins.

Later, Paul referred to his former way of living as the "old man of sin" (Rom. 6:6). He said he used to be "a blasphemer, a persecutor, and an insolent man [i.e., a violent opponent of Christianity]" (1 Tim. 1:13), but he obtained God's mercy and grace when he obeyed the gospel. He was a new man!

BECOMING NEW

Some people were hesitant to believe Paul had really changed. They accused him of pretending to be a Christian so he could destroy Christianity from the inside. He addressed those accusations in 2 Corinthians 5. The Lord gave Paul a new life, and that newness was evidenced in three ways. We, too, will demonstrate our newness in these same three ways.

1. Paul emphasized the eternal.

In 2 Corinthians 5:9-11, Paul said that this life is not going to last forever. Christians are looking forward to being with the Lord. "[W]e make it our aim, whether present or absent, to be well pleasing to Him" (2 Cor. 5:9). This requires a shift in our perspective. Just a few verses earlier, Paul put it this way:

> While we do not look at the things which are seen, but at the things which are not seen. For the things which are seen are temporary, but the things which are not seen are eternal (2 Cor. 4:18).

Life on Earth is important, but it is not most important. We should use this life to prepare for eternal life in Heaven (Eccl. 12:13)! That is how you emphasize the eternal.

2. Paul was controlled by Christ.
Paul said he was controlled by the love of Christ (2 Cor. 5:14, ESV). "Control" in that verse literally means "to be held together." In other words, Paul's life was held together by Christ's love. That's what him motivated to live for Jesus.

> [Jesus] died for all, that those who live should live no longer for themselves, but for Him who died for them and rose again (2 Cor. 5:15).

In 1 Corinthians, Paul said, "you are not your own" (1 Cor. 6:19). He would go on to say, "For you were bought at a price; therefore glorify God in your body and in your spirit, which are God's" (1 Cor. 6:20). The price that was paid to purchase you was the blood of Jesus (1 Pet. 1:18-19).

Stop for a minute and think about that phrase: "you are not your own." That's new. When we were in sin, we basically served ourselves, conducting ourselves "in the lusts of our flesh, fulfilling the desires of the flesh and of the mind" (Eph. 2:3). Now we belong to Jesus.

This concept is further illustrated in 1 Corinthians 12, where Christians are referred to as individual "members" of Christ's body (1 Cor. 12:27). This means that we are His arms, legs, feet, eyes, mouth, and so on. Jesus is called "the head of the body" (Col. 1:18). He controls His body, telling it what to do.

Being a "member" of the church is not like being a member of a country club. Rather, being a member of the church means that I am an active agent of Jesus today. Christ's love for me motivates me to obey Him, and, by my obedience to His word, the Lord controls my life.

3. Paul recognized spiritual realities.

The way Paul looked at others had changed. Notice how he explained it in 2 Corinthians 5:16-17:

> Therefore, from now on, we regard no one according to the flesh. Even though we have known Christ according to the flesh, yet now we know Him thus no longer. Therefore, if anyone is in Christ, he is a new creation; old things have passed away; behold, all things have become new.

To "regard [someone] according to the flesh" means to evaluate someone based on external features. Paul was more interested in a person's soul.

* * * * *

How would Paul see you? *First*, he would see you as one who is "in Christ." Saying that someone is "in Christ" is the same as saying that someone is a Christian. Galatians 3:27 says, "For as many of you as were baptized into Christ have put on Christ." When you were baptized, you were placed in Christ (Eph. 1:13).

Second, Paul would say that you are "a new creation." When you came up out of the waters of baptism, you rose to "walk in newness of life" (Rom. 6:4). The "old you" was "crucified with [Jesus], that the body of sin might be done away with, that [you] should no longer be [a slave] of sin" (Rom. 6:6). That's why Paul said, "old things have passed away" (2 Cor. 5:17). The meaning is that the old has, once and for all, ceased to exist. Now "all things have become new." It means the new has come to stay! So, when you read that anyone who is in Christ is "a new creation" (2 Cor. 5:17), you know that it applies to you!

The new in you began when you were forgiven of your past sins through baptism (Acts 2:38; 22:16). This "newness," however, extends past the baptistery, affecting your entire life.

A CLOSER LOOK

Having thought about how Paul would look at you, now let's consider how you look at other people. Paul said he did not want to think of anyone "according to the flesh" (2 Cor. 5:16). You should work to think that way, too. The idea is that you are to change the way you think about *everything* – to the point of reconsidering how you view others. You should strive to see people through the eyes of Jesus.

Would Jesus show partiality to people because of their gender, their race, or their income? We know that He wouldn't because He didn't while He was on Earth. Instead, He spoke with a Samaritan woman (the Jewish culture hated the Samaritans, John 4:9), and visited Zacchaeus in his home (Zacchaeus, a chief tax collector, was likewise hated by the Jewish culture of Jesus' day, Luke 19:7). These are two of many examples that illustrate Jesus' heart. He said, "[T]he Son of Man has come to seek and to save that which was lost" (Luke 19:10). That's how Jesus viewed people: saved or lost, right with God or away from God. And Jesus came to help them all.

A Christian's standards for interacting with someone are not rooted in what brand of clothes they wear, the color of their skin, the neighborhood in which they reside, or whether they have a "blue collar" or a "white collar" job. We see people for what they are – the focus of God's love (John 3:16), and, therefore, worthy of our time in providing them a positive influence for Jesus (compare Matthew 22:39).

Chapter 2
A NEW GOAL

ONE DAY AT A TIME

Day Eight – Colossians 3:1-4
1. Where is Christ?

2. Where should we focus our minds?

Prayer Starter – Pray about heaven. Thank God for His promise that you can go there.

Day Nine – Matthew 6:19-21, 24
1. Describe heavenly treasures. Contrast them with earthly treasures.

2. What does it mean to lay up treasures in heaven?

Prayer Starter – Thank God for your material blessings (money, possessions, your income that enables you to pay your bills). Pray for strength to use these things for God's glory.

Day Ten – Mark 12:28-31
1. How should we love God?

2. Make it practical. How do you do what this text commands?

Prayer Starter – Thank God for showing you His love. Be specific in the ways He has shown His love to you.

Day Eleven – Philippians 3:12-21
1. Where is our citizenship?
2. Whom do we eagerly await?

Prayer Starter – Thank God for accepting you His holy citizen in His kingdom.

Day Twelve – 1 Thessalonians 4:13-18
1. When Jesus comes, who will rise first?

2. After them, then who?

Prayer Starter – Thank God for His assurance that the faithful who have died will not be forgotten.

Day Thirteen – Revelation 21:1-4
1. "The tabernacle [dwelling place] of God is with _____."

2. How is Heaven described in this passage?

Prayer Starter – Praise God for His design of Heaven. Specifically mention each "no more" from Revelation 21:4.

Day Fourteen – 1 John 2:15-17
1. What should we not love?

2. What will happen to the world?

Prayer Starter – Ask God to help you focus more on Him and less on things.

BRINGING IT ALL TOGETHER

Not all of the effects of the new in you are visible to the physical eye. Only a spiritual perspective can appreciate what Jesus has done *for* you in saving your soul and what He can do *through* you in blessing the lives of others. To see things from a spiritual point of view does not take a graduate degree in theology. All it takes is a willingness to allow Heaven and eternity to shape your view of our physical existence.

Imagine you are standing in front of a full-length mirror. The mirror is old and heavy, encased by an ornate golden frame. It looks like a treasure you would find in your grandmother's attic. You can't resist walking up to it and taking a look. As you examine the image in the reflection, you quickly notice that this mirror is unlike any other you have ever seen. The mirror doesn't show a *physical* reflection, but a *spiritual* one. Just like an X-ray shows you a picture of the inside, so this spiritual mirror exposes the infirmities of the soul.

Realizing the special nature of the mirror, you jump back, closing your eyes and looking away in fear of what you might see. Then, slowly, you sneak a quick glimpse – only opening one eye at first, then the other.

This is not the first time you have stood before this mirror. The last time you were here was not a pleasant experience. It was when you were first learning the gospel. You were horrified to see the sin that covered your soul, staining it red like crimson (Isa. 1:18). The more you learned about the gospel, the more you noticed your heart was being touched – even pierced – with its convicting power (Heb. 4:12; Rom. 1:16). It was a wakeup call for your life. The image, though difficult to view, was exactly what you needed to see in order to fully appreciate that the blood of Jesus could heal you.

Today, you find yourself before the mirror once again. This is a regular spot for Christians who are mindful of 2 Corinthians 13:5: "Examine yourselves as to whether you are in the faith." You hesitantly approach. Like a patient waiting for the doctor to reveal the results of a test, you are both excited and scared to death to see the reflection in the mirror. You finally work up the courage to look, and you are shocked by what you see.

"All of the stains – they're ... *gone!*" you exclaim.

Tears stream down your cheek as the joy of your salvation floods your soul. You erupt in praise to God as you fall to your knees in reverent prayer.

What Jesus has done to cleanse your soul from the stains of your sins cannot be overstated. At the same time, it cannot be adequately described (Paul calls it God's "indescribable gift," 2 Cor. 9:15). The cleansing is *real*. The change is *real*. The newness is *real!* You are different now. You are *the new you*.

QUESTIONS

1. Why is it so difficult to live in preparation for eternity?

2. What does it mean to be controlled by the love of Christ?

3. What motivated Paul's radical change from persecuting Christians to pleasing Christ?

4. Describe how Jesus viewed other people. Why must you work to see other people like He did?

5. What place does Jesus occupy in your life? Do you elevate other relationships above your relationship with Him?

ACTION ITEMS

1. *Recognize spiritual realities.* Make a list of people you know who do not know Jesus.
2. *Think eternally.* Make congregational Bible study and worship a priority – this week and every week.

WHAT'S NEW?

The greatest asset to your success as the new you is your focus. When Jesus said, "seek first the kingdom of God and His righteousness" (Mat. 6:33), He was talking about focus. Further, when the Lord stated that the first of all the commandments is to "love the LORD your God with all your heart, with all your soul, with all your mind, and with all your strength" (Mark 12:30), He was talking about focus.

Christian focus is shaped by Christian goals. The clearer your focus on Christian goals, the more faithful you will be. In Colossians 3, Paul describes the new goal of the new you.

> If then you were raised with Christ, seek those things which are above, where Christ is, sitting at the right hand of God. Set your mind on things above, not on things on the earth (Col. 3:1-2).

Here are some questions you must answer: – When I get where I am going, where will I be? What am I working toward? What is my goal? Colossians 3:1-2 will help you shape your focus, which will help you identify your new goal as a Christian.

BECOMING NEW

1. Understand the significance of your baptism.

The Colossians to whom Paul wrote had been baptized. Paul said they "died with Christ," (Col. 2:20) and were "buried with [Jesus] in baptism" (Col. 2:12). Additionally, they "were raised with Christ…" (Col. 3:1). This death, burial, and resurrection was a reference to their baptisms.

The act of immersion represents the old you dying to your sins. Going completely under the water represents the burial of the old you. There is a spiritual significance to the act of going under the water because, according to Romans 6:3, "we were buried with [Jesus] through baptism into death." Baptism connects us with Jesus' death and the blood He shed on the cross.

Dying and being buried with Jesus was not easy, was it? It required taking a long, hard look at who you used to be before you became a Christian. As you studied God's word, you were shown the consequences of your sins, ultimately resulting in hell! Spiritually speaking, that version of you needed to die. You were forced to admit wrongs and confront fears. Perhaps you had to confront the fear of hearing something totally different from what you had heard before. Maybe there was a fear in telling friends or family members that you were going to be baptized. Maybe the fear involved making a decision in front of a whole congregation of people.

The old you went down into the water, but the new you came up out of the water! The act of coming up from the water after immersion signifies our connection to Christ's resurrection. Paul said, "[J]ust as Christ was raised from the dead by the glory of the Father, even so we also should walk in newness of life" (Rom. 6:4). Yes, it was difficult to admit wrongs and confront fears, but it was worth it! You were raised with Jesus! You have a brand new life! But what now?

2. Seek Christ.

Paul said Christians "seek those things which are above" (Col. 3:1). That is your new goal. But what does it mean? "Things above" refers to Heaven. While Heaven is a spiritual realm (therefore, it cannot be referred to in terms of geography), the Bible often describes it as being "up." For example, John 3:13 says that Jesus "came down from heaven." Verse twelve of that chapter says that Jesus spoke of "heavenly things." As Christians, our citizenship is in Heaven (Phil. 3:20), which means that Heaven is our home – not this world. We are not to be focused on the physical things, but on the eternal (2 Cor. 4:17-18). Our focus is on Heaven.

A Christian's goal is not simply going to Heaven; the goal is to be "where Christ is" (Col. 3:1). Think about it: if your primary motivator for wanting to go to Heaven is so that you can be with Christ, then that truly changes things. Can you imagine what it will be like to be in the very presence of your Savior? Think back to the feelings that preceded your baptism (what you wrote on pages 11-12). How did the guilt of your sin make you feel? Think about what you felt when you realized that you hurt your Heavenly Father and sent Jesus Christ to the cross. Then, think about how you felt after your baptism. What a glorious contrast! Jesus is the one who made that drastic change possible! Focus on Jesus.

Notice where Paul said Jesus is – "sitting at the right hand of God" (Col. 3:1). This is a place of honor and privilege. Jesus went there when He ascended back to Heaven (Acts 2:32-33; 7:56; 1 Pet. 3:22).

If you are really serious about your new goal of seeking Christ in Heaven (and I hope you are), then consider your life from Jesus' perspective on the throne. See your life how He sees it. What on this earth is worth losing your relationship with Christ? What is here that is worth going to hell?

Here is my point: the fact that you are now a Christian will not make temptation go away. In fact, your battle with sin likely will only intensify as you continue to grow in Christ. So, when you are tempted, focus on Jesus and where He is. Evaluate your decisions based upon whether something will bring you closer to Him or push you further from Him.

3. Dedicate your thoughts to heavenly things.

The path to embracing your new goal of seeking Christ in heaven begins in your mind. The mind is often called the heart in Scripture (the idea is that the heart is where one's thoughts, reasonings, and emotions reside). Your thoughts are on display in what you do. If you want to see Christ in Heaven, then you must begin to think about Him now. Daydream about seeing Jesus. Think about how much He loves you (1 John 3:16), and what it will be like to see Him as He is (1 John 3:2). Think about the fact that He is your friend (John 15:13). He knows your name

(John 10:14)! He provides for all of your needs (see Psalm 23). How could we not spend time thinking about Him?!

In Colossians 3:2, Paul contrasts "things above" and "things on the earth." He is contrasting "things that are only subordinate and instrumental (things of earth) and things that are supreme and final (things of heaven)."[1] Physical things ("things on the earth") are certainly blessings from God (James 1:17), but they are not ends; they are means to an end. We should use the things on the earth to glorify God and help improve our relationship with Him. Look at how Paul referred to people who focused too much on earthly things:

> For many walk, of whom I have told you often, and now tell you even weeping, that they are the enemies of the cross of Christ: whose end is destruction, whose god is their belly, and whose glory is in their shame—who set their mind on earthly things (Phil. 3:18-19).

Allow God, through His word, to shape your thoughts, values, and loves. The only way you can accomplish this is by focusing on Him and on His will for your life.

A CLOSER LOOK

The word *seek* in Colossians 3:1 actually means "to go about, desire, endeavor, inquire." Think about it like a mother whose three year old son slipped away from her sight while they were at the grocery store. When she realizes her little boy is gone, nothing will prevent her from locating her child. She is *seeking* her child.

When Christ was born (incarnated), Herod, the ruler, was jealous of the Child because he heard that people were calling the Child "the King of the Jews" (Mat. 2:2). Herod evidently felt that his authority was threatened. Matthew 2:13 says that Herod was

---

[1] Weaver, Walton. *Truth Commentaries: Philippians and Colossians.* Bowling Green, KY: Guardian of Truth Foundation, 1996. Print.

seeking the young Child to destroy Him. Herod would not rest until he had found Jesus so he could kill Him. The word that is used in Matthew 2:13 (and again in verse 20) is the same word used in Colossians 3:1.

As Herod sought to kill Jesus, the Bible says that someone is seeking *you*. He comes to you "to steal, to kill, and to destroy" (John 10:10). Look carefully at 1 Peter 5:8:

> Be sober, be vigilant; because your adversary the devil walks about like a roaring lion, seeking whom he may devour.

Satan is "seeking" to spiritually harm you. He intends to reverse all of the good that Jesus has done in your life. He will convince you to do evil so you will lose your soul in hell. You have come too far to allow the devil that kind of access to your soul! The price that redeemed your soul is too precious to go back now (1 Pet. 1:18-19).

To fight off the enemy, you must put into practice what Paul instructed in Colossians 3:1. *Seek* heavenly things; *seek* Christ. Long for Him, desire Him, turn over every stone looking for Him. Open your Bible and learn of Him (Mat. 11:28-30). There is a wealth of Biblical treasure just waiting for you to explore.

BRINGING IT ALL TOGETHER

Jesus said, "Blessed are those who hunger and thirst for righteousness, for they shall be filled" (Mat. 5:6). If you have ever tried to maintain a healthy eating plan, then you know how difficult it can be to change your appetite. There are things that you will crave, but you can't have them if you want to stay faithful to your diet.

The new you is about changing your interests to seek Christ. It's like changing your appetite. Christians want what Christ wants for their lives. They want to love what Jesus loves and hate what Jesus hates. This will require them to stop loving some things and to start loving other things. Our world will tell you it is impossible to change your spiritual appetite, but it is not. You can do it by changing your focus.

Not only is Jesus the reason you are the new you, He is the goal of the new you! So "hunger and thirst for righteousness," and "seek those things which are above." Make living for Christ your main goal, and you will become an even stronger new you!

QUESTIONS

1. How did baptism connect you to Jesus?

2. What is the connection between your thoughts and your goal?

3. In what ways has Satan been tempting you? What is his goal?

4. How does Matthew 5:6 relate to your Christian goal?

5. How will you "seek" things that are above?

ACTION ITEMS

1. *Change your appetite.* Identify one part of your life that is not leading you to your new goal. What can you do this week to change that and seek righteousness?
2. *Means to an end.* How can you use your physical blessings (i.e., your house, your car, your computer, your social media accounts, etc.) to glorify God?

Chapter 3
A NEW LIFE

ONE DAY AT A TIME

Day Fifteen – Colossians 3:1-4
 1. Now that you have died, where is your life hidden?

 2. When Christ appears, what will Christians do?

 Prayer Starter – Thank God for giving you new life through His Son.

Day Sixteen – Romans 6:1-11
 1. "We were _____ with Him through baptism…"

 2. "We should walk in _____ ____ _____."

 Prayer Starter – Thank God for the blood of Jesus, which cleansed you at your baptism.

Day Seventeen – Reread Romans 6:1-11
 1. What happened to our "old man"?

 2. Who has been "freed from sin"?

 Prayer Starter – Thank God for freeing you from the slavery of sin.

Day Eighteen – 1 John 3:1-8
 1. Why doesn't the world know us?

 2. What does "everyone who has this hope" do?

 Prayer Starter – Thank God for the love He has shown you in allowing you to be His child.

Day Nineteen – 1 John 5:11-15

1. Where is eternal life found?

2. Why did John write these things?

Prayer Starter – Thank God for giving you confidence in your salvation.

Day Twenty – Romans 8:12-18

1. As children of God, we are also "_____ _____ with Christ."

2. The sufferings of this present time cannot compare to what?

Prayer Starter – Thank God for sufferings, which provide opportunities to grow closer to Him.

Day Twenty-One – Philippians 2:5-11

1. One day, every knee will bow to _____.

2. Will this include those who are unbelievers?

Prayer Starter – Pray that the Lord will use you to share the gospel with those who have not yet obeyed it.

WHAT'S NEW?

Pretend for a minute that everything you have ever heard about the church and Christianity is written on a huge white board. This would include everything the Bible teaches, but also everything that the world believes about those topics. Now, take the imaginary eraser and remove it all.

Do you have a nice, clean board? Good!

Now write Colossians 3:3-4 on that clean board. Here's what it says:

> For you died, and your life is hidden with Christ in God. When Christ who is our life appears, then you also will appear with Him in glory.

If that verse was all you knew about the church, you would be missing a lot of the great truths from other passages in the Bible, but you would at least know this: Christianity is a lifestyle. Paul said, "Christ … is our life." That's huge. If Christ is my life, then I'm going to live for Him every day, not just on Sunday.

See, our culture views Christianity as if it's something you can "put on" and "take off," kind of like the "Sunday best" that you wear to worship. If you are with certain people, you will be your most "Christian" self. If you're with others, you may let it slide. That is not what Christ wants for you.

The Bible teaches that, before we became Christians, we "were dead in trespasses and sins" (Eph. 2:1). But God "made us alive together with Christ" when we obeyed His will (Eph. 2:5). Romans 6:4 puts it this way: we rose from the waters of baptism to "walk in newness of life." When you obeyed the gospel and became a Christian, you not only received a new goal, you also accepted a new life.

BECOMING NEW

1. You are the walking dead.
Colossians 3:3 describes people who died, but also were alive. Paul said, "For you died, and your life is hidden with Christ in God." In Galatians 2:20, Paul said that he had been crucified with Christ. Then he said this: "It is no longer I who live, but Christ lives in me." The death to which Paul referred was his baptism (Romans 6:1-4). Earlier in Colossians, Paul reminded these Christians that they "died to the basic principles of the world" (Col. 2:20).

The emphasis of being "dead, but alive" in the New Testament is supposed to get us to think differently about our lives. Now that you are a Christian, you are only alive because Christ made you alive. Remember, you were "dead in trespasses and sins." Such a state is exactly what you earned because "the wages of sin is death" (Rom. 6:23). However, God's rich mercy and love motivated Him to send His Son to die in your place (John 3:16). Today, you are spiritually alive – and it's all because of Jesus! Your life belongs to Him.

The fact that your life belongs to Jesus is more than a simple, good-sounding phrase. It is a characteristic of the new you that must be displayed in every part of your life. Every decision must be made in view of service to the Lord. That is why Paul concluded Galatians 2:20 this way: "the life which I now live in the flesh I live by faith in the Son of God, who loved me and gave Himself for me." The "old you" died, and Christ now directs the new you.

2. Not everyone will get it.
The fact is, most people will think you're weird for following Jesus (1 Pet. 4:3-4). They may label you as "radical" or say that you are "taking it too far" while you attempt to follow Jesus in every facet of your life. Paul addressed this with the Colossians when he said, "your life is hidden with Christ in God" (Col. 3:3). When Christ appears, we also will "appear with Him in glory."

There is an interesting contrast between the word "hidden" in verse 3 and the second instance of the word "appear" in verse 4. What is hidden? "Your life is hidden" (Col. 3:3). Paul was referring to your new life in Christ – the new you. From whom is your life hidden? It is hidden from a world that rejects Christ. Here is the point: people who are not New Testament Christians just don't get it.

Think about some of the Christian attitudes that are portrayed in Scripture. The "Golden Rule" (Mat. 7:12) directs us to treat others the way they should treat us. Romans 12:17 says that we should not seek vengeance on those who harm us. Paul said he found contentment and strength in Christ – even when he suffered for Christ (Phil. 4:11-13). In 2 Corinthians 4:17, Paul called the difficulties in his life temporary, "light afflictions." He also stated that his present sufferings were not worthy to be compared with the glory that he would enjoy in heaven (Rom. 8:18).

How can Christians have these kinds of attitudes? How can they face adversity with faith, trial with triumph? People who don't have a relationship with Christ do not understand these types of attitudes because they do not have what we have: a new life in Christ. Our new life is motivated to seek Christ above all else (Col. 3:1-2, as we studied in chapter two). We know that, even if something bad happens to us here, we get to be with Jesus in Heaven after this life is over. Isn't that amazing?! Today, though, the goal of the Christian life is hidden (concealed, secret) to those who are unwilling to hear and heed the gospel.

One day, it won't be hidden anymore. Jesus will appear in the clouds to gather His disciples and take them to the home that He has prepared for them (John 14:1-6). At that moment, those who have rejected Christ will no longer be able to deny Him. Everyone will acknowledge Him as Lord; every knee will bow to Him and every tongue will confess Him as the Son of God (Phil. 2:10-11). On that day we will "see Him as He is" (1 John 3:2). The righteous will be divided from the unrighteous, and, in that moment, we will "appear with Him in glory" (Col. 3:4). The effect and importance of our Christian lives will no longer be "hidden." Everyone will know to Whom we belong.

3. Christ is everything.

Colossians 3:4 says, "Christ ... is our life." You should be careful not to compartmentalize Christ to only a portion of your life. It seems like many religious people want to put Jesus and the church into a box that is only accessed on Sundays. The New Testament, however, calls on you to make Christ your life. Nothing is excluded from that. I've heard Dan Winkler, one of my favorite preachers, say, "Jesus shouldn't just occupy first place in your life. Jesus should BE your life." Jesus is everything.

A CLOSER LOOK

Let's take a closer look at the day when Jesus will appear. While Christ is at the right hand of God today (Col. 3:1-2), the day will come when Christ will appear (Col. 3:4). The Bible has a lot to say about this day.

First, no one knows when this day will come (Mat. 24:36). Attempts to predict the day are futile.

Second, the Lord Himself will descend from Heaven and appear in the clouds (1 The. 4:16). That is why it is sometimes called the "Second Coming of Christ." Note that the Bible does NOT say that Jesus will come and reign on the Earth for a period of time (His kingdom, which is the church, has already been established, Mat. 16:18-19. You are in it! [as were the Colossians, Col. 1:13]).

Third, faithful Christians who have already died will be raised from the dead (1 The. 4:16). Then, faithful Christians who are still alive when Jesus comes will rise to meet the Lord in the air (1 The. 4:17). Going to be with the Lord is the victory which Christians await (John 14:1-6)! This victory, which faithful Christians will receive that day, is possible only through Jesus (1 Cor. 15:57).

Fourth, every person who has ever lived will be there and will be judged for everything he or she has done, whether good or bad (2 Cor. 5:10). People of all nations will be present, and will be separated into two categories: the righteous and the unrighteous (Mat. 25:31-46). The righteous will be permitted into Heaven for eternity; the unrighteous will be sentenced to eternity in Hell. That is why this day is sometimes called "Judgment Day."

Because "flesh and blood cannot inherit the kingdom of God," (1 Cor. 15:50), our bodies will be changed (1 Cor. 15:51). We must be changed from our fleshly bodies because Heaven is a spiritual realm rather than a physical one. We do not know how those new bodies will look. John said that "it has not yet been revealed what we shall be" (1 John 3:2). We will be changed rapidly, in the blink of an eye, at the sounding of "the last trumpet" (1 Cor. 15:52).

Fifth, the New Testament teaches that Jesus' appearing in the clouds will initiate the destruction of the physical universe. Peter addressed this in 2 Peter 3:10:

> But the day of the Lord will come as a thief in the night, in which the heavens will pass away with a great noise, and the elements will melt with fervent heat; both the earth and the works that are in it will be burned up.

Sixth, we should note that this judgment is final and eternal.

If you are like me, you would like to know a lot more about the Judgment Day. However, I would encourage you to remember two extremely important things. First, that will be the day when "we shall see Him as He is" (1 John 3:2). We will see Jesus on the Judgment Day! Second, we must always be prepared for that day. "Even so, come, Lord Jesus" (Rev. 22:20)!

The new you will be ready. Your entire life is consumed in Jesus! On the day He comes in the clouds, your faith will become sight and your hope will be realized. What a day that will be!

BRINGING IT ALL TOGETHER

The old you was dead in sin, but Christ created the new you through the rebirth of baptism (John 3:3, 5)! You were raised from spiritual death and given new life in Jesus! Don't squander that gift. Don't allow the shiny, tempting things of the world to distract your focus and derail your life for the Lord. Use every moment to live for Jesus. He expects no less.

> Then He said to them all, "If anyone desires to come after Me, let him deny himself, and take up his cross daily, and follow Me" (Luke 9:23).

QUESTIONS

1. Why is it so necessary for you to change from your old self in order to faithfully live for Christ?

2. How is a Christian's spiritual life "hidden"?

3. What are some Christian attitudes that the world finds strange?

4. Make a list that describes, in order, what will take place on the Judgment Day.

5. How might some people "compartmentalize" Christ to a portion of their lives?

ACTION ITEMS

1. *The walking dead.* What died? When you became a Christian, the old you died and the new you rose to live for Christ. What has changed? In what can you no longer participate?
2. *Your hidden life.* Prepare a kind, godly response to this comment: "So you think you are the only one going to heaven?"

Chapter 4
A NEW ENEMY

ONE DAY AT A TIME

Day Twenty-Two – Genesis 3:1-6
1. Why was it sinful for Adam and Eve to eat the fruit from the tree in the midst of the garden?
2. How did Satan change what God had said?

Prayer Starter – Pray for God to help you not to be led into temptation.

Day Twenty-Three – 1 John 3:4-10
1. How does this passage define sin?
2. Why was Jesus manifested?

Prayer Starter – Ask God's blessings on you as His child. Pray that your life will please Him.

Day Twenty-Four– James 4:1-10
1. What will happen if we resist the devil?
2. If we draw near to God, what will happen?

Prayer Starter – Thank God that He allows you to have a relationship with Him.

Day Twenty-Five– Philippians 3:14-21
1. What was Paul's emotional reaction to those who lived in sin?
2. How did Paul describe their relationship to Christ?

Prayer Starter – Pray for those who are enemies of the gospel, that their hearts might be touched by truth and that they will repent of their sin.

Day Twenty-Six– Ephesians 6:10-20
1. Why does Paul instruct Christians to put on the whole armor of God?

2. "Having done all, to _____."

Prayer Starter – Ask God for courage to withstand temptation.

Day Twenty-Seven– Reread Ephesians 6:10-20
1. How is Satan described in these verses? What kinds of weapons does he use?

2. List the different pieces of the armor of God. How do you think each one is used?

Prayer Starter – Thank God for His warnings about Satan and sin. Thank Him for equipping you with His armor so you can remain faithful to Him.

Day Twenty-Eight – Romans 5:6-11
1. Describe our spiritual state before we were saved by Jesus.

2. Describe our spiritual state after we contacted Christ's salvation.

Prayer Starter – Thank God for saving you through Jesus.

WHAT'S NEW?

You have a target on your back. In a way, it has always been there. He's been watching you your whole life. However, your recent decisions have only made him watch you even closer. It's foolish to think you can hide from him. He is relentless, and will stop at nothing. He will exploit your closest friends, turning them against you. He will attack at your most vulnerable moments, waiting for you to let your guard down.

This creepy description isn't the beginning of an episode of *Law and Order* or *Criminal Minds*, it is the true story of what Satan is doing to you. The devil is real. He's always wanted you to be spiritually dead and doomed to hell, but, now that you're a Christian, he will only intensify his pursuit of you.

For this lesson, we will briefly leave Colossians 3 and focus on one verse from 1 Peter:

> Be sober, be vigilant; because your adversary the devil walks about like a roaring lion, seeking whom he may devour (1 Pet. 5:8).

BECOMING NEW

Satan is your new enemy. Yes, he has been pursuing you all along, but now you have changed. You have a new goal and a new life that are opposed to Satan. Just as he is intent on pursuing you, you must be committed to fleeing and fighting him. From 1 Peter 5:8, we will notice three observations that will help you win your battle with the devil.

1. Let's be honest about sin.

I want to deal with this in two sections. *First,* I want to simply point out that, from the fleshly perspective, sin can be fun in the moment. If you were given the choice between suffering and pleasure, which one would you choose? We would naturally want pleasure more than pain, right? That's the fleshly perspective. The spiritual perspective, however, causes us to ask this question: "At what cost does the pleasure come?" Hebrews 11:25 says that Moses chose "to suffer affliction with the people of God than to enjoy the passing pleasures of sin." This exposes an important truth. Sin's pleasures are passing. They will cause you to lose your soul to Satan.

Second, sin's pleasures are nothing but lies. The word "Satan" means *slanderer*. He's basically a professional liar. He deceived Eve with a lie (Gen. 3:1-6), and continues to deceive men and women today. Sometimes he is even successful at deceiving Christians. Paul said that the devil "transforms himself into an angel of light" (2 Cor. 11:14), pretending to be something he's not for the sake of convincing Christians to abandon their faith.

Some in the New Testament "turned aside to Satan" (1 Tim. 5:15). Carefully consider this fact: Satan could deceive you, too.

There is nothing appealing about sin when you see it from the spiritual perspective. The Bible deems a person who lives in sin as an enemy of God and as one who is under Satan's sway. Judas, who betrayed Jesus and gave Him over to the angry mob, is said to have done this because the devil put it into his heart (John 13:2; compare Luke 22:3). Ananias and his wife, Sapphira, lied about some money in an effort to appear more generous than they actually were. Peter exposed the lie and asked Ananias, "[W]hy has Satan filled your heart to lie…?" (Acts 5:3).

John wrote, "He who sins is of the devil" (1 John 3:8). He went on to say that you can distinguish between a child of God and a child of the devil by the way he or she acts (1 John 3:10).

Ultimately, Satan will be punished for what he has done in leading a prideful rebellion against God (compare 1 Timothy 3:6-7). Sadly, those who have been deceived by the devil will be sentenced to hell, "the everlasting fire prepared for the devil and his angels" (Mat. 25:41).

Your adversary the devil walks about (1 Pet. 5:8). Satan is real. So let's be honest about Satan's deceptions: there is nothing pleasurable about sin.

2. Satan wants to take you down with him.

The devil is not blind to the punishment that he has earned from God. Revelation 12:12 says "he knows that he has a short time." His goal now is to make you fall away from God so that you will go to hell, too. 1 Peter 5:8 says that Satan is "like a roaring lion, seeking whom he may devour."

Satan will do all he can to stop the work of God's people (Mat. 13:24-30, 36-43). Jesus told a story in which He depicted the devil as stealing the word out of people's hearts (Luke 8:11-12). He would cause some of the Christians in Smyrna to be imprisoned for their faith (Rev. 2:10). One day when Jesus was telling His disciples about His nearing crucifixion and subsequent resurrection, Peter, trying to defend the Lord, told Jesus, "Far be it from You, Lord; this shall not happen to You!" (Mat. 16:22). Jesus responded,

> Get behind Me, Satan! You are an offense to Me, for you are not mindful of the things of God, but the things of men (Mat. 16:23).

Jesus responded that way because He knew it was God's will for Him to die on the cross for the sins of the world (Mat. 1:21). Peter was actually standing in the way of God's will. If Jesus had not gone to the cross, all people would be eternally lost in sin. That is exactly what the devil desires; he wants everyone to go to Hell.

Satan would love to stop Christians from taking the message of salvation to the world. The gospel is lost humanity's only hope (Rom. 1:16).

The devil will be punished for his deeds, and he wants to take you down with him.

3. You must take action.

Peter says, "Be sober, be vigilant" (1 Pet. 5:8). To be sober means to control yourself. You can't allow passing pleasures to deceive you into swapping your soul's salvation for sin. You must watch for your enemy ("be vigilant") and be prepared to face his attacks with faith and commitment to God.

I recently saw a news story about a mountain lion that was loose in California.[1] The news website has helicopter footage of the mountain lion walking around the campus of John F. Kennedy high school in Granada Hills. Later, it jumped a wall and went into someone's yard! What would you do had you been in Granada Hills, California that day? If you knew about that mountain lion, you would have stayed inside until you knew for sure that it was safe to go back out! You would probably watch out the window for the animal. I'm sure you wouldn't try to go outside and see if you could get close enough to pet it. You would be sober and vigilant for your safety.

Here's what we know: Satan is actually seeking you like a lion pursuing its next meal. He wants to attack you and kill you (John 10:10). Millions of people (including some Christians, I'm sad to say) go about their lives as though the lion is not there. Still others, aware of the lion's presence, live as though they want to get as close to the lion as possible without actually touching it. Some seem to want to pet it. That's not how you win your battle with Satan. You won't go to heaven like that.

Ephesians 4:27 says that we should not "give place to the devil." The old saying goes, "If you give the devil an inch, he will become your ruler." It's true. You must "resist the devil" so that "he will flee from you" (James 4:7). The only way to do that is by suiting up in the "whole armor of God, that you may be able to stand against the wiles of the devil" (Eph. 6:11).

Here's my point: you won't win the war for your soul unless you are proactive about it. Take actions *right now* to be sure you are not "taken captive by him to do his will" (2 Tim. 2:26).

A CLOSER LOOK

I want you to know that you really can win against Satan. The reason you stand a chance is because of Jesus. The Bible is clear:

---

[1] "Mountain Lion on the Loose in California." WTVT. Fox13news.com, 16 Apr. 2016. Web. 28 Apr. 2016.

> ## THE WHOLE ARMOR OF GOD
>
> *The belt of **truth*** – In ancient times, the belt held together the other parts of the armor. Likewise, the truth girds the Christian's defenses against Satan's attacks. We must LEARN truth (2 Tim. 2:15), and we must APPLY truth (Psa. 119:11).
>
> *The breastplate of **righteousness*** – The breastplate covered from the neck to the waist. Righteousness is right living. Satan, whose names means *accuser*, cannot accuse the Christian who is covered with a godly life (1 John 3:7, 10)!
>
> *The sandals of preparation of the **gospel of peace*** – The sandals of Romans soldiers had hobnails on the soles (like cleats) in order to be prepared to fight. Similarly, living the gospel and sharing the gospel (Rom. 10:15) prepares us to be victorious over our enemy.
>
> *The shield of **faith*** – The shield was a full-body covering. It would thwart arrows and defend the soldier who carried it. Your faith ("unshakable trust in undeniable fact"[2]) will extinguish the devil's fiery arrows.
>
> *The helmet of **salvation*** – Satan wants to attack your mind (2 Cor. 11:1-3) through intellectual and rationalistic doubt. The assurance of our salvation will help us fight (1 John 2:3-5; 5:13).
>
> *The sword of the Spirit, which is **the word of God*** – As a sword, God's word (Rev. 2:16; Hosea 6:5) is powerful (2 Cor. 10:4-5), pricking (Acts 2:36-38), piercing (Heb. 4:12), and penetrating (Acts 7:54).
>
> We are to put on this armor with *persistent **prayer*** (Eph. 6:18).

Jesus has already won the victory for those who belong to Him. Hebrews 10:12-13 says this of our Lord:

> But this Man, after He had offered one sacrifice for sins forever, sat down at the right hand of God, from that time waiting till His enemies are made His footstool.

Jesus came to earth, taking upon Himself the form of a servant, to "destroy him who had the power of death, that is, the devil, and release those who through fear of death were all their lifetime subject

---

[2] Caldwell, C.G. *Truth Commentaries: Ephesians*. Bowling Green, KY: Guardian of Truth Foundation, 1994. Print. 315.

to bondage" (Heb. 2:14-15). Jesus' victory is promised to those who have been cleansed by His blood. Paul told the Christians in Rome that "the God of peace [would] crush Satan under [their] feet" (Rom. 16:20).

While Satan is a formidable foe, he is no match for Jesus Christ! If you maintain your focus on seeking Jesus and living for Jesus, then you will overcome your new enemy.

> But thanks be to God, who gives us the victory through our Lord Jesus Christ (1 Cor. 15:57).

BRINGING IT ALL TOGETHER

Seeing Satan and sin as your enemy will take a shift in your thinking at first. This is part of repentance. The key is to realize that the things the "old you" used to do (the things that were sinful) are the very ways that Satan is trying to attack you. You are spiritually alive in Christ (Eph. 2:5), but the devil wants you to be spiritually dead.

This will require a lot of introspection. Take a long, hard look at your soul. As you do, pay close attention to the things that tempt you to sin. Realize that the consequences of those sins may not be immediately apparent; there may be some things that you are tempted to do that only you would know about. Nevertheless, those sins have very real – and very eternal – consequences.

After you have thought for a while about the ways that Satan tempts you, make a list of those vulnerabilities on a piece of paper. Writing them down will help keep them before your mind so that you don't let your guard down. Plus, you can use this list to pray that God will give you strength in these areas. You don't have to show this list to anyone if you don't want to, however I would encourage you to find a fellow Christian in whom you can confide, and let him or her know that these are areas in which you struggle. Ask them to be your accountability partner, checking in with you periodically to see how you are doing. Ask them to pray for you in your temptations. Ask them if they have any tips for overcoming temptation (after all, they are tempted by things just like you are).

Remember that there is a roaring lion on the loose, and there is a target on your back. Be faithful. Resist Satan. Maintain your focus on the faith and you will find the way of escape (1 Cor. 10:13).

QUESTIONS

1. Why are some things righteous and other things sinful?

2. How does the cross of Christ make us victorious over sin?

3. What is Satan's goal?

4. What can we do to protect ourselves from Satan's temptations?

5. What are the consequences of giving in to temptation?

ACTION ITEMS

1. *Be proactive.* Develop a plan for resisting temptation. Write it on an index card or save it to a note on your phone for easy access when you are being tempted. Tweak your plan as necessary for it to be most effective.
2. *Accountability partner.* This week, sit down with a Christian and ask him or her how he or she fights Satan. Ask for helpful verses of Scripture and helpful prayers that they pray. Ask them how they avoid tempting situations.

Chapter 5
A NEW STANDARD

ONE DAY AT A TIME

Day Twenty-Nine – Colossians 3:5-10

1. What are we to do with our earthly members?

2. Why is "passion" included in this list? Isn't it good to be passionate about something?

Prayer Starter – Pray for God to help you be pure in heart and body. In your private prayers, be specific in asking God for help in the areas in which you need to improve.

Day Thirty – 2 Thessalonians 1:6-12

1. When the Lord comes, on whom will He take vengeance?

2. What will happen to them?

Prayer Starter – Pray that lost souls will obey the gospel before it is too late. In your prayer, mention specific names of lost souls whom you know.

Day Thirty-One– 2 Peter 3:9-12

1. From verse 9, why hasn't the Lord returned yet?

2. What is the answer to Peter's question in verse 11?

Prayer Starter – Thank God for His patience with mankind.

Day Thirty-Two – Reread Colossians 3:5-10

1. If the sins in Colossians 3:5 are sexual sins, what kind of sins would you say are listed in verses 8 and 9?

2. What are we to do with these types of sinful activities?

Prayer Starter – Pray for God to help you be pure in speech. Confess ways that you do not use your tongue as you should.

Day Thirty-Three – James 3:1-6

1. To what does James compare the tongue?

2. "The tongue is a _____ member and boasts _____ things."

Prayer Starter – Pray for God to help you to be more mindful of controlling your tongue.

Day Thirty-Four – James 3:7-12

1. No man can _____ the tongue.

2. About what does James say, "these things ought not to be so"?

Prayer Starter – Pray that your words may please God and glorify His name.

Day Thirty-Five – Psalm 19:7-14

1. How does the psalmist describe God's word?

2. What is his prayer at the end of this psalm?

Prayer Starter – Use Psalm 19:14 to construct a sentiment that you can pray today.

WHAT'S NEW?

A man – we'll call him Jim – called the church office one day and asked if he could stop by and chat. A few minutes later, he was sitting in the chair on the other side of my desk.

"I have been reading the Bible," Jim said, "and I have decided that I want to be baptized."

I was elated! Jim and I had known each other for a long time. He had never been much of a religious person, but recent events had caused him to think about his soul, which sent him searching the pages of the New Testament.

He and I discussed what it means to be a Christian (a lot of which is what we studied in the first few chapters of this book). Then Jim said something I'll never forget.

"I understand that being a Christian means I have to change my life," he explained. "After all, Christians are called to a much higher standard. I can't keep living the way I used to live and be a Christian."

I was privileged to assist Jim in baptism that day.

Jim was exactly right. Christians are called to a much higher standard. That standard is not merely a set of expectations that "non-church goers" have for "church goers." The bar is set in Scripture, and – I should warn you – the bar is pretty high.

> Therefore put to death your members which are on the earth: fornication, uncleanness, passion, evil desire, and covetousness, which is idolatry. Because of these things the wrath of God is coming upon the sons of disobedience, in which you yourselves once walked when you lived in them. But now you yourselves are to put off all these: anger, wrath, malice, blasphemy, filthy language out of your mouth. Do not lie to one another, since you have put off the old man with his deeds (Col. 3:5-9).

BECOMING NEW

Colossians 3:5-9 sets the standard for how we should live. There are three things we should notice about this passage.

1. Some things simply cannot stay.

Verses 5 through 9 contain two sets of lists. The first is in verse 5 and the second is in verses 8 and 9. Notice that verse 5 and verse 8 begin similarly: "Therefore put to death…" (Col. 3:5), and "But now you yourselves are to put off all these…" (Col. 3:8).

I don't know about you, but I really don't like spiders. My wife and I happen to live in an environment perfect for banana spiders. Go ahead, do a quick Google image search for "Banana Spiders" … if you dare. When we first moved to South Carolina our back yard had five or six of them in different spots. At the risk of sounding like less of a man, it was terrifying.

One day, we stepped out of the front door, onto the front porch to find that one of these beasts had spun a web overnight, blocking the step off of the porch to get to the driveway. There it was, in all of its yellowy nastiness, blocking our exit. My wife happened to find a large piece of stone that she hurled onto the spider. The stone fell to the ground and the giant spider was trapped underneath.

When Paul says, "put to death your members which are on the earth" (Col. 3:5), he means to pitilessly slay, much like my wife and I did with the nasty banana spider. You have to cut all ties with the ways of the world and with the sinful activities of the "old you."

Now, imagine that you put your coat on in the winter time and realize that one of those terrible banana spiders is in your sleeve! What will you do? If you're like me, then you'll get that coat off as fast as possible and throw it all the way across the room. *That's* exactly what Paul means when he says, "put off all these" (Col. 3:8). Remove sinful things, just like you would remove a coat with a spider in it.

Physical acts of impurity have no place in a Christian's life.

Notice that the five sins listed in verse 5 are sexual sins. Paul lists fornication, uncleanness (impurity), passion (sinful, sensual emotions), evil desire (violent lust), and covetousness (trying to get something [or someone] that isn't yours). This list could not be more relevant to our culture, which is consumed with sensuality.

Additionally, verbal acts of impurity have no place in a Christian's life. The five sins listed in verse 8 are sins of speech: anger (an outburst of temper), wrath (anger boiled up and turned into a vengeful rage), malice (the evil intentions of one who is angry against another), blasphemy (speech directed against the good character of someone else), and filthy language (abuse in foul language). Verse 9 adds lying to this list.

These two lists of sins indicate the higher standard to which you are called. The eleven sins listed in these verses are all attributes of the *old* you; they have no place in the life of the new you.

2. God will punish wickedness.

In verse 6, Paul explains why you must remove these sins from your life.

> Because of these things the wrath of God is coming upon the sons of disobedience.

Punishment of wicked behavior is sure to come. On the Judgment Day, God will punish those who persist in sin (which we discussed in the chapter two).

Remember that God's punishment of wickedness is not arbitrary. God is just, and sin deserves punishment. Further, God's holiness will not allow Him to be in the presence of sin. Therefore, on Judgment Day, God will eternally separate Himself from the people who refused the forgiveness He offered them through the blood of Christ (2 The. 1:7-10). Habakkuk 1:13 says that God is "of purer eyes than to behold evil, and cannot look on wickedness." Sin cannot enter God's presence.

3. These Christians were formerly involved in these sins.

The book of Colossians was originally written to Christians who lived in Colossae (Col. 1:2). These Christians were normal people, just like you and me. Before they became Christians, they had been involved in the very sin Paul had just listed in verse 7.

The Bible is designed to challenge our thinking and call us to a higher standard. 2 Timothy 3:16-17 says that God's word teaches us the right way (it is profitable for doctrine), points out when we're going the wrong way (it is profitable for reproof), tells us how to correct our path (it is profitable for correction), and encourages us to stay on the right way (it is profitable for instruction in righteousness).

Fighting sin won't be easy. In fact, it will be a constant struggle. Even people who have been Christians for half a century continue to fight sin and struggle with temptation because temptation is common to all men (1 Cor. 10:13). Don't give in to the "passing pleasures of sin" (Heb. 11:25). Remember that you are called to a higher standard, God's standard. The Christians in Colossae could do it, and you can, too!

A CLOSER LOOK

Sometimes the truth is hard. It is not difficult to understand, but it can be hard to practice. The Bible calls us to a high standard, and living by that standard is not always easy. Sin must be removed, and we must seek holiness. Not only does God call us to be holy (1 Pet. 1:15-16), He promises to punish those who do not heed His warnings. Many people in our politically correct culture would find that offensive.

Consider this: does God have the right to offend you? To state it another way, will you grant God access to your heart so that He can continue to mold it through His word, or will you get mad at God for identifying sin in your life and commanding you to change?

Jesus told a story about a sower (Mat. 13:1-9, 18-23; Luke 8:4-8, 11-15). The seed that this man sowed fell on four types of soil: wayside, stony, thorny, and good soils. Jesus then revealed that the four types of soils represented four types of hearts, and the seed represented God's word.

The wayside soil illustrated a closed heart. It refused to think, felt that it had no room for improvement, and chose to reject the truth rather than receive it.

The stony soil illustrated shallow faith. It accepted truth initially, but quickly abandoned it when things became difficult.

The thorny soil illustrated a crowded mindset. Like the stony soil, the thorny heart accepted the truth at first, but was ultimately too busy with other things to pay attention to the truth.

The good ground, of course, illustrated a heart that willingly listened and obeyed.

Which one of these soils describes your heart? The fact that you are working through this book tells me that your heart is a "good ground" type of heart. However, you must be careful, for your heart could change at any moment if you do not closely watch it.

If you will live up to the standard of the new you, then you must give God access to your heart.

BRINGING IT ALL TOGETHER

When we became Christians, the Lord added us to His church (Acts 2:47), which is His kingdom (Mat. 16:18-19). God "delivered us from the power of darkness and conveyed us into the kingdom of the Son of His love" (Col. 1:13). The word "church" means "called out." The new you has been *called out* of the sin in which you used to participate. Get rid of, put to death, anything that is inconsistent with the new that Christ created in you.

QUESTIONS

1. Why is covetousness listed among sexual sins?

2. What is malice?

3. List four ways the Bible is profitable to us.

4. Discuss how we as the church live out the definition of being the "called out."

5. What are the consequences of failing to practice truth?

ACTION ITEMS

1. *Put it to death.* At the end of each day, take a few minutes to think through your day and write down the areas in which you fell short. Literally write them in a notebook. The list is for personal use only. There is no reason to show it to anyone unless you choose to do so. This will help you to be mindful of avoiding these things in the future. Continue this practice as long as you need to turn from those activities.
2. *Does God have the right to offend you?* Jesus often preached truths that were difficult to hear. Study Luke 14:25-35 and list Jesus' teachings that are easy to understand, but difficult to put into practice.

Chapter 6
A NEW IDENTITY

ONE DAY AT A TIME

Day Thirty-Six – Colossians 3:9-11
1. How does verse 10 describe "the new man"?
2. Think about the phrase "Christ is all in all." What does it mean?

Prayer Starter – Thank God for the opportunity to be new, cleansed from your sins.

Day Thirty-Seven – Galatians 3:26-29
1. Those who have "put on Christ" are those who were _____ _____ _____.
2. What does "for you are all one in Christ Jesus" mean?

Prayer Starter – Thank God for the unity we enjoy in Christ.

Day Thirty-Eight – Romans 12:1-2
1. In what ways are we to present ourselves before God?
2. How are we transformed? Where does the transformation take place?

Prayer Starter – Pray that those who conform to the sinful practices of the world will turn to the truth, and pray that you will not allow yourself to conform to the world.

Day Thirty-Nine – Ephesians 4:20-24
1. Where does the renewal take place?

2. How was the new man created?

Prayer Starter – Pray that God will purify your heart so you can be renewed for Him.

Day Forty – 1 Peter 2:1-3; 2 Peter 3:17-18
1. What are new Christians ("newborn babes") supposed to desire? Why?

2. In what are we supposed to grow?

Prayer Starter – Thank God for the ability to grow in Christ. Pray for wisdom as you grow in your faith.

Day Forty-One – Colossians 1:12-15
1. Where is deliverance from the power of darkness found?

2. Jesus is the image (or, manifestation) of Whom?

Prayer Starter – Thank God for revealing Himself to you through His word and through His Son.

Day Forty-Two – 1 John 4:7-12
1. If God so loved us, we should do what?

2. How can we know God abides in us?

Prayer Starter – Pray that God will help you to show His love to everyone you meet.

WHAT'S NEW?

Webster defines identity as "the distinguishing character or personality of an individual: individuality."[1] Your identity is who you are.

Christianity demands one hundred percent of yourself. God expects you to love Him with your all (Mark 12:29-30), holding nothing back from the Lord (Gal. 2:20). When you became a Christian, you took on a new identity. Paul stated it this way in Colossians 3:9-11:

> Do not lie to one another, since you have put off the old man with his deeds, and have put on the new man who is renewed in knowledge according to the image of Him who created him, where there is neither Greek nor Jew, circumcised nor uncircumcised, barbarian, Scythian, slave nor free, but Christ is all and in all.

BECOMING NEW

Do you see the change in identity from these verses? At the end of verse 9, Paul said that "you put off the old man with his deeds." When the old you was "put off," so were your former actions. In the place of the old, you "put on the new man" (Col. 3:10). The new could not come until the old was removed. The old you and the new you cannot coexist.

We are talking about a total change in your identity. You have a new goal of seeking Christ, and a new life that revolves around Him. There is no time to waste, because your new enemy is pursuing you. You must measure up to your new standard, ridding your life of things that are inconsistent with the new in you. You have been recreated! Forgiven of your past sins, you are now changing from the inside out.

This is not to say that you need to become a robot, void

---

[1] http://www.merriam-webster.com/dictionary/Identity

of your unique personality. God created you with a unique personality and skill set. When you merge your personal talents with the new you in Christ, God will use you to accomplish great things for His glory (Mat. 5:16)!

Notice three important observations about your new identity.

1. Christians are a work in progress.

According to Colossians 3:10, the new man is under construction. The word "renewed" means "to renovate."

Do you watch the show on TV where they take an old house and make it look like new? In thirty minutes or an hour, the host of the show and his or her team guts a house and makes it look like a totally different place. From my couch, that job looks pretty quick and easy. However, in real life, renovation is a long, hard process. Months of hard work are poured into that structure. Tears erupt and arguments ensue when the budget of $5,000 turns into $15,000 – all because the electrical work had to be stripped and totally upgraded (I think I've seen too many of these shows).

Renovation isn't easy. Some parts are smooth, but other parts are very hard. According to Paul, that's the Christian life. The new you is a work in progress. It's OK that you don't know everything yet. You aren't expected to know it all; you just started this journey. However, it will not be OK if, ten years from now, you hardly know more than you know now (Heb. 5:12-14).

All of this renovation takes place in your mind. Ephesians 4:23-24 tells you to "be renewed in the spirit of your mind, and ... put on the new man." Romans 12:2 says to "be transformed by the renewing of your mind." In our text, Paul said the new man is renewed "in knowledge" (Col. 3:10). In other words, you need to learn more about God's word to be new. All Christians are expected to "grow in the grace and knowledge of our Lord and Savior Jesus Christ" (2 Pet. 3:18).

The Bible discusses our spiritual growth in terms of our physical growth. You were born a baby (everyone I know was).

Babies can't eat meat; they have to begin on milk and work their way up to solid food. The same is true for new Christians. When you were baptized, you were "born again" (John 3:3, 5). You are a spiritual baby. "As newborn babes, desire the pure milk of the word, that you may grow thereby" (1 Pet. 2:2).

Babies don't grow if they aren't fed, and you won't grow as a new Christian if you aren't fed. In fact, if you don't regularly study from God's word, not only will you not grow, but the new you will not survive.

This growth does not happen overnight, and you will never know all there is to know about the Bible. That is why we say Christians are a work in progress.

2. Your new identity has Christ's "fingerprints."

You are renewed in knowledge "according to the image of Him who created" you (Col. 3:10). Jesus is Who created you. Christians are conformed to the image of God's Son (Rom. 8:29). We are being transformed into His image (2 Cor. 3:18). Our new identity means that, when people see us, they should see someone who thinks like Jesus (Phil. 2:5), talks like Jesus (1 Pet. 2:22), and acts like Jesus (1 Cor. 11:1; 1 Pet. 2:21).

Obviously, there is a difference between an identity and a mask. Some people try to fake Christianity, but that is a path to failure. Genuine renewal will lead you down a path of deep, meaningful transformation and will introduce you to an intimate relationship with Jesus. Paul summarized it this way: "Christ is all and in all" (Col. 3:11). He is absolutely everything.

3. We're all in this together.

I don't know who said it, but it's true: "the ground is level at the foot of the cross." The meaning is that everyone is in equal need of the salvation made possible by the cross – regardless of race, culture, gender, or social class. In Christ, "there is neither Greek nor Jew, circumcised nor uncircumcised, barbarian, Scythian, slave nor free, but Christ is all and in all" (Col. 3:11).

That verse naturally breaks into three categories. *First,* Christ brings *racial* unity. There is "neither Greek nor Jew" in Christ. All Christians are brothers and sisters in God's family. *Second,* Christ brings *cultural* unity. The contrast between circumcised and uncircumcised denotes the strong emphasis that many were still placing on the Jewish practice of circumcision. The Law of Moses in the Old Testament called for circumcision. The New Testament, however, does not have such a mandate. Circumcision bears no religious significance today. In spite of our different cultural backgrounds, we can all unite as New Testament Christians. *Third,* Christ brings *social* unity. Paul said that there is neither "slave nor free" in Christ. The idea is that Christians of different social classes can care for each other and treat one another with Christ-like kindness (Eph. 4:32).

We could add Galatians 3:28 to Colossians 3:11 for a *fourth* observation: Christ brings unity among *genders.* In Christ, "there is neither male nor female" (Gal. 3:28). This does not negate the fact that men and women have different roles in the home and in the church. However, we must remember that women were severely devalued in ancient cultures. The gospel elevated women to a status equal with men – just as God created them (Gen. 2:21-24).

No Christian should become haughty, as if he or she is "better" than any other Christian. Though we are all different from each other, we are united in this fact: we are all here because of Jesus. "Christ is all and in all." Jesus has erased our differences and unified us, working toward the same end in the life of each Christian. We must honor this fact by the way we treat each other.

A CLOSER LOOK

It's a shame that there is so much division in our culture, but it is no surprise. That's what happens when Satan influences the human heart. Jesus came to unite us in one body (Eph. 4:4), His church (Eph. 1:22-23).

Sometimes, however, we continue to be divided – even in our assemblies. How can we accentuate our new identity in Jesus and be truly united?

Here are five ways that we can achieve that kind of unity.

1. We will all get along when we see each other as God sees us. God sees value in each person. "He fashions their hearts individually; He considers all their works" (Psa. 33:13-15).

2. We will all get along when we value each person as an immortal soul. This goes back to having an eternal perspective. Jesus said that every person is a soul, and that an individual soul is worth more than the riches of the whole world (Mat. 16:26).

3. We will all get along when we unite on the only standard that will bring us together. Paul wrote to a divided church and begged them to "speak the same thing" so that there would be no divisions among them (1 Cor. 1:10). He wanted them to be "perfectly joined together in the same mind and in the same judgment." Christian unity is possible only when we all agree to follow God's word.

4. We will all get along when we realize that "God shows no partiality" (Acts 10:34). If we wish to please Him, then we won't show partiality, either.

5. We will all get along when we humble ourselves enough to love and forgive others. Everyone makes mistakes. When someone hurts us, we should treat them with kindness and mercy, as we would want them to treat us (Mat. 7:12). We should have a forgiving spirit, as Christ did (Eph. 4:32).

Ultimately, it takes the very thing that Paul mentioned in Colossians 3:11. Christ must be all and in all; He must be absolutely everything. When everyone is focused on Christ first, the new you will truly shine for God's glory.

BRINGING IT ALL TOGETHER

The journey of the new you began the moment you were raised with Christ in baptism (Rom. 6:4). God redeemed you by the blood of Christ, and your past sins were forgiven. Now, your journey continues as you grow and are transformed in your thoughts and deeds to be more like Jesus.

The extent of your transformation is entirely up to you. As we have seen, God wants it to be a complete change. He has given you a new identity that is wrapped up in the name that you wear – CHRISTian (note the emphasis on Jesus).

This new identity is not a burden, it is a blessing. The task of the new you is to grow closer and closer to Jesus, falling more and more in love with Him. "His commandments are not burdensome" because we love Him (1 John 5:3). Embrace your new identity and live the life of the new you, the best life ever.

QUESTIONS

1. Describe your new identity.

2. How can God use your personality and skill set to bring Him glory?

3. What barriers has Christ broken to create unity among His disciples?

4. Explain the meaning of "Christ is all and in all."

5. Why is haughtiness a threat to the unity of the church?

ACTION ITEMS

1. *Knowledge is power.* Having a good, working knowledge of God's word is vital to your transformation as the new you. Take this week to memorize the names of all 66 books in the Bible in order (Genesis to Revelation). If you have already done that, then select a Bible verse (or a few verses) to memorize this week.
2. *Be the solution, not the problem.* This week, seek out a brother (if you are a man) or a sister (if you are a woman) who is different from you, and work to get to know them better. Go to lunch, play golf, have coffee, help them with something — do *something* to get to know them.

Chapter 7
A NEW FAMILY

ONE DAY AT A TIME

Day Forty-Three – 1 John 3:13-18
1. Does God's love abide in the person described in verse 17? Why or why not?
2. What does it mean to love "in deed and in truth"?

Prayer Starter – Pray that God will help you live your love and not just speak it.

Day Forty-Four – Ephesians 2:1-10
1. What is being described in verses 4-6?
2. Through whom did God show the riches of His grace?

Prayer Starter – Thank God for grace, His gift that we could never deserve.

Day Forty-Five – Philippians 2:3-8
1. Describe how we should treat each other from verses 3 and 4.
2. Who is the greatest example of these qualities?

Prayer Starter – Ask God to help you have the mind of Christ.

Day Forty-Six – 2 Corinthians 10:1-6; Matthew 5:1-12
1. How does Paul describe Jesus?
2. What is the reward for meekness?

Prayer Starter – Pray for the strength to be meek.

Day Forty-Seven – 1 Corinthians 13:1-8
1. What is the first description given about love (1 Cor. 13:4)?

2. What does that mean?

Prayer Starter – Pray for patience.

Day Forty-Eight – Ephesians 4:25-32
1. Who is meant by "one another" in verse 32?

2. How should we forgive each other?

Prayer Starter – Thank God for forgiving you, and pray that He will help you forgive others.

Day Forty-Nine – Colossians 3:8-14
1. To what does the word "therefore" (in verse 12) connect?

2. How does Paul describe love in this passage?

Prayer Starter – Pray that God will give you the strength to put off sinful things and the courage to put on qualities of holiness.

WHAT'S NEW?

It's really easy to *read* about the total transformation of the new you, but it is very hard to actually change. The new in you does not come without effort. Your new lifestyle will be the result of intentionality, prayer, study, and diligence to seek Christ and obey God. That's a tall order for you to accomplish by yourself.

Stop and reflect on the day you were baptized. Flip to the front of this book and review your answers from when you told me about your baptism. Do you still feel the same enthusiasm and passion as you did that day? Honestly, now that you are almost fifty days in to the new you, some of it may have waned. That is not unusual. In fact, it is very common.

The problem is, we don't have time to let the fire die out. It's clear that the Lord expects us to be "all in." Your goal is to be in Heaven, where your Savior is, and you better believe your enemy is not easing up on you (1 Pet. 5:8). He wants you to lose your passion, to leave "your first love" (Rev. 2:4).

So how will you keep your spiritual fire burning?

The answer is — You won't.

I've seen it too many times: people become Christians and are on fire for the Lord ... for a week or two. Then, I stop seeing them at worship services. I try to get in touch with them, but they won't return my calls or reply to my email. Just like that, they're gone.

You won't do it alone, and here's why: God didn't design Christianity to be done alone. He has equipped you with one of the greatest blessings on earth, His family.

> Therefore, as the elect of God, holy and beloved, put on tender mercies, kindness, humility, meekness, longsuffering; bearing with one another, and forgiving one another, if anyone has a complaint against another; even as Christ forgave you, so you also must do. But above all these things put on love, which is the bond of perfection (Col. 3:12-14).

These verses teach us how to access the resources of God's family.

BECOMING NEW

1. Appreciate the blessings of Gods family.

Christians are God's people, we are "of God" (Col. 3:12). This links us together as a family. Throughout the book of Colossians, Paul referred to his family in the Lord. His dear friend and protégé, Timothy, is called "our brother" in Colossians 1:1, and Paul referred to his friend, Tychicus, as "a beloved brother" in Colossians 4:7. Onesimus, the runaway slave from the book of Philemon who became a Christian, is likewise called a "beloved brother" (Col. 4:9). We'll have more to say about these individuals in chapter 12, but for now notice that they were Paul's brothers in the Lord.

In Colossians 3:12, Paul used three descriptions to refer to God's family. *First,* he said that Christians are "the elect of God." Some translations say, "God's chosen ones" (ESV). Since before the creation of the world, God's plan has been to save His people by the precious blood of Christ (1 Pet. 1:18-20). In so doing, God would create a people "who once were not a people but are now the people of God, who had not obtained mercy but now have obtained mercy" (1 Pet. 2:10). Inasmuch as the gospel is for all (Rom. 1:16), God's family is open to all people (Acts 10:34-35). This is God's wonderful family!

Second, Paul describes God's people as "holy," which means "set apart." To be holy means that we have been cleansed from our sinful impurities and that we are doing our best to remain clean from sin's stains. Peter wrote, "as He who called you is holy, you also be holy in all your conduct" (1 Pet. 1:15). Later, when he wrote about the Judgment Day when the universe will be destroyed, he asked, "[S]ince all these things will be dissolved, what manner of persons ought you to be in holy conduct and godliness…?" (2 Pet. 3:11). God's family is holy.

Third, Paul describes Christians as "beloved" (Col. 3:12). The term expresses God's deep, abiding love for His children. Christians are "in Christ" (Gal. 3:26-27), and Jesus is God's "beloved Son" (Mat. 3:17). Christians, therefore, are "accepted in the Beloved" (Eph. 1:6). As members of God's family, we are "beloved brethren" (1 Thes. 1:4).

It is the greatest of honors to be in God's family!

2. Build Christian relationships.

Having identified and described our relationship to each other, Paul mentions a series of things that Christians should "put on" (Col. 3:12). This contrasts with the things that we were to "put off" in Colossians 3:9. Notice that the transformation process of the new you is about more than what we *should not* do, it also involves things we *should* do. You might clean out your closet by removing everything inside, but then something has to be put back in it.

When you contacted Jesus' blood at your baptism, you were totally cleansed from your past sins. Now you are doing your best to fully remove the sinful elements that remain, but you must also fill your life with good things.

Each of the characteristics mentioned in Colossians 3:12-13 have to do with how we treat each other in God's family. Verse 12 deals with characteristics of the *heart*, while verse 13 deals with characteristics of our *actions*.

First, we have characteristics of the heart. Christians are to "put on" five attitudes. "Tender mercies" refer to having a sympathetic heart, exhibiting heartfelt compassion for your fellow Christians. "Kindness" is a goodness of heart that motivates you to serve one another in love (the "kindness" of "God our Savior" toward us is what cause Him to send His Son to die for us, Titus 3:4). "Humility" is a lowliness of mind that focuses on others rather than being absorbed with yourself. If we realized our unworthiness and had more affection and sympathy for our brethren, there would be less fault finding, grudge holding, fussing and fighting among God's people. In the Bible, "meekness" is strength under God's control, submitting our actions and our emotions to God. Meek does not mean weak, nor does it mean the absence of anger (see Eph. 4:26), it simply means that your emotions, words, and actions will be placed under God's control. "Longsuffering" is patience, and would involve a willingness to endure mistreatment.

All of these traits of the heart are to be "put on" and never removed (such is the thrust of the word in the original language). This command for permanent action means you never have God's permission to be harsh, cold, short-tempered, or haughty.

Second, Paul listed characteristics of our actions. We are to "bear with one another." This is the outward demonstration of patience ("longsuffering" from verse 12). We are to be "forgiving," which means we should not hold on to bitterness or grudges. It is never right to refuse forgiveness to someone who lovingly seeks it. "[A]s Christ forgave you, so you also must do" (Col. 3:13). We are to forgive as Christ forgave. Once again, we see the standard is very high. If a Christian has a problem with another Christian, they are to work it out and get over it. Notice from the verse that it does not matter whether there was a justified reason for the complaint, the point is to work toward a speedy resolution. This will only work when Christians are eager to ask for and to grant forgiveness.

The character traits listed in verse 13 originate from the right kind of heart (described in verse 12). Without the right heart, the right actions will not exist.

3. Above all, put on love.

Colossians 3:14 sets love apart from the foregoing characteristics. This is because love is necessary for each of these qualities to exist in a Christian. Love is a characteristic of both the heart and the actions. This love seeks the highest good of its object. It is the kind of love that resulted in God giving "His only begotten Son" for us (John 3:16).

Love binds relationships together. Paul said that love "is the bond of perfection." The word "bond" is referring to the relationship that we have in Christ; it solidifies that relationship in unity.

Further, love builds relationships, helping them to mature. The word "perfection" refers to a mature, complete relationship. Love is a powerful force. No wonder Paul said he was nothing without love (1 Cor. 13:1-3).

A CLOSER LOOK

Did you know that you were chosen by God? Here's how it happened. Before God created the world, He knew that human beings would fall to sin (God knows everything, Isa. 46:10). However, God had a plan for redeeming His sinful creation. It was God's perfect will that Jesus would come to earth and die as a sacrifice for us. He would take our place in death for our sins and would endure the punishment that sin brings upon us (1 John 2:2). Jesus was "foreordained before the foundation of the world" (1 Pet. 1:20).

It was God's plan (again, before the world was even created) that He would call people to salvation. This would be accomplished by the message of the gospel (2 The. 2:14). By obeying the gospel, people would become "holy and without blame before Him in love" (Eph. 1:4), and would be adopted "as sons by Jesus Christ" (Eph. 1:5). They would be "conformed to the image of His Son, that He might be the firstborn among many brethren" (Rom. 8:29). Romans 8:30 wraps it up for us:

> Moreover whom He predestined, these He also called; whom He called, these He also justified; and whom He justified, these He also glorified.

Let's break down that verse. God predestined (knew ahead of time) that those whom He called (by the gospel, 2 The. 2:14) would be justified (rendered as righteous, guiltless) by their obedience of that message (Rom. 6:17). Therefore, they would be "glorified," raised up from the mire of sin and elevated as God's children (Eph. 1:5)!

Here's my favorite part of this – that's *you!* You are "the elect of God." When you chose to obey the gospel and give your life to serving and obeying the Lord, you submitted to a plan that has been in place since before time began. By doing so, you were united with hosts of others – in the past, present, and, Lord willing, in the future – who are also God's "elect." The elect of God are those who submit to His plan by obeying His will. This is God's amazing family!

BRINGING IT ALL TOGETHER

You can't live the life of the new you all by yourself. Sure, your faithfulness is still your responsibility, but God has given you a wonderful support system in your family. It is my prayer that this book, humbly written by your brother in Christ, can provide you with some of that familial support.

Don't miss an opportunity to be with your family in Christ when they assemble together. God's people meet each Sunday to worship God and to encourage each other (Heb. 10:24-25). Many congregations will also meet at some point during the week for further fellowship and Bible study. Additionally, most congregations periodically have activities that provide opportunities to enjoy one another's company and to get to know each other better. Don't miss these opportunities. You need that encouragement from them, and they need that encouragement from you.

Finally, I do not want you to lose the big picture of God's family. In Christ, you are connected to a group of believers much larger than the number of Christians who live in the same place you do. You have a familial relationship to New Testament Christians all over the globe! More than that, you are now connected to all of God's people who have lived and who will live. Rejoice in this!

You do not have to live as the new you all alone. In fact, God does not want you to! He has given you a loving, supportive family with whom you share the goal, the life, the enemy, the standard, and the identity of the new you.

QUESTIONS

1. Explain the phrase, "elect of God."

2. What is the relationship between right actions and a right heart?

3. Why is love placed "above all" the rest?

4. What can you do to improve your relationship with and get "plugged into" your Christian family?

5. Make a list of some ways that Satan may tempt you to stay home on Sundays instead of going to worship with God's family.

ACTION ITEMS

1. *A global family.* Get the contact information for a missionary that your congregation supports, and write a note to encourage him and his family. After all, they are your brothers and sisters in Christ!
2. *A family member in need.* Do you know a brother or sister in Christ who is sick, facing surgery, recovering from surgery, grieving, or struggling in some other way? Serve them this week. Write a card, make a call or a visit, take them a meal. Let them know you care about your family in Christ.

Chapter 8
A NEW HEART

ONE DAY AT A TIME

Day Fifty – Colossians 3:15-17
   1. What are we to let the peace of God do?

   2. What are we to let the word of Christ do? How?

   Prayer Starter – Thank God for His peace in your life.

Day Fifty-One – John 17:14-21
   1. If "these alone" refers to Jesus' disciples (those who were in His presence as He prayed), to whom does Jesus refer when He prays for "those who will believe" (John 17:20)?

   2. "That they all may be _____ ... that they also may be _____ in Us."

   Prayer Starter – Pray for unity among God's people, and that you will be in harmony with God's will.

Day Fifty-Two – Ephesians 2:11-18
   1. Who is our peace?

   2. When He came, what did He preach?

   Prayer Starter – Thank God for the blood of Jesus, which has brought us nearer to Him.

Day Fifty-Three – Philippians 4:6-13

1. Instead of being anxious, what should we do?

2. How does Paul describe God's peace?

Prayer Starter – Pray for something that is worrying you. Be specific. Give it to God and let Him handle it.

Day Fifty-Four – Ephesians 5:15-20; reread Colossians 3:16

1. When we sing, we are "_____ and _____ one another."

2. When we sing, we are to make melody in our _____ to the _____.

Prayer Starter – As you pray today, praise God that He is worthy of worship. Pray that your worship to Him this Sunday honor and please Him.

Day Fifty-Five – Matthew 7:21-29

1. What must one do in order to go to heaven?

2. The one who was told to depart from Jesus was the one who did what?

Prayer Starter – Thank God for revealing His will, the way to heaven.

Day Fifty-Six – Reread Colossians 3:15-17

1. What does the Holy Spirit command us to do twice in these verses?

2. What does it mean to let God's peace and Christ's word dwell in our hearts?

Prayer Starter – Spend your time in prayer thanking God for as many blessings as you can count.

WHAT'S NEW?

When the Bible speaks about the heart, it is most often discussing the inner-most part of you, including your thoughts, feelings, decisions, and morality. It is no surprise, then, that God's word would expect the new you to have a change of heart, because the Bible was designed to penetrate "the thoughts and intents of the heart" (Heb. 4:12).

As we noticed in chapter six, the transformation of your new identity begins in your mind, that is, in your heart. In fact, it began when "you obeyed from the heart that form of doctrine to which you were delivered" (Rom. 6:17).

If you don't pay close attention to your heart, you will reduce your faith to empty actions, void of thought, feelings, and understanding. For example, some Christians lose the meaning of worship because they lack the "spirit" (John 4:24), or the heart, of worship. Others find it difficult to fully commit to the strict guidelines of God's standard because they lack heart. Your faith must be deep and rich, touching every part of you, especially your thoughts, emotions, and decisions.

Your new heart is very important to the new you. Paul addressed that new heart in Colossians 3:15-17

> And let the peace of God rule in your hearts, to which also you were called in one body; and be thankful. Let the word of Christ dwell in you richly in all wisdom, teaching and admonishing one another in psalms and hymns and spiritual songs, singing with grace in your hearts to the Lord. And whatever you do in word or deed, do all in the name of the Lord Jesus, giving thanks to God the Father through Him (Col. 3:15-17).

BECOMING NEW

It is nearly impossible to overstate the importance of your heart in living as the new you. From the text before us, we will notice three observations about your new heart.

1. Spiritual success is rooted in your new heart.

In this passage, Paul references "the peace of God" (verse 15), "the word of Christ" (verse 16), and "the name of the Lord Jesus" (verse 17). In each instance, he offers us inspired guidelines for our hearts.

First, the peace of God should **rule** your heart. Only God can impart this kind of peace. It "surpasses all understanding" (Phil. 4:6-7), and is only available to disciples of Jesus (John 14:27). It both calms the individual soul (Phil. 4:6-7) and brings people together (Eph. 2:14-18).

That peace is to "rule in your heart" (Col. 3:15). The word "rule" means to govern or umpire. While war rages within us over Satan's temptations (1 Pet. 5:8), the presence of God's peace adjusts the conflicting passions of the worldly versus the spiritual and helps us to make the right decision. This is not a miraculous thing; it works to the extent that you allow God's peace to rule your heart. As always, the choice is your's.

Second, the word of Christ should **reside** in your heart. Jesus is both the source and the subject of the gospel message, therefore it is called "the word of Christ." This word is to "dwell in you richly" (Col. 3:16). You should allow God's word to take permanent residence in you, being brought completely under its influence. The psalmist identified this as a strategy to ward off sin:

> Your word I have hidden in my heart,
> That I might not sin against You (Psa. 119:11).

It is to reside in you "richly," which means "in abundance." You can't obey something that you don't know. Neither can you defend something with which you are not familiar. You cannot share the message of the gospel unless you know that saving message. God's word must reside in abundance in your heart.

Third, the name of the Lord should **regulate** your heart. Nothing is omitted from that phrase "whatever you do" in verse 17. Everything must be done in the name of the Lord. That word,

"Lord," means "owner, possessor, one having authority." To do anything in His name is to do it by His authority. Everything you do should be in accordance with God's law. Remember that the very definition of sin is to break God's law (1 John 3:4).

If your heart is a place where God's peace rules, Christ's word resides, and the Lord's authority regulates, then you will know spiritual success.

2. Worship flows from your new heart.

Paul addressed worship in Colossians 3:16. When he mentioned "teaching and admonishing one another in psalms and hymns and spiritual songs," he was clearly referring to a worship assembly (they could sing to one another because they were assembled in worship). That being the case, notice the correlation between "the word of Christ dwelling in you" and "singing with grace in your hearts to the Lord." Worship is an expression of your heart.

This verse clearly commands singing as a means of expressing our worship to God. Notice four important observations about singing from Colossians 3:16. *First,* the heart is the only instrument used in our singing in worship. To sing is "to use your voice to make musical sounds in the form of a song or tune."[1] There is no authority in Scripture for singing in worship to be accompanied by instruments. Since everything we do is to be done by the Lord's authority (Col. 3:17), and the Lord does not authorize instrumental music in worship, we must conclude that to use such would be sinful. *Second,* every Christian is to participate in the singing. When Christians are singing, they are "teaching and admonishing one another" through the songs. How can you obey this command if you are not singing? *Third,* the messages of the songs must be biblical. We are told to sing "psalms, hymns, and spiritual songs," which refer to songs with sacred themes. By mentioning "spiritual songs," God's word eliminates the use of secular songs (including patriotic songs)

---

[1] http://www.merriam-webster.com/dictionary/sing

from worship. *Fourth,* we are singing "to the Lord." He is the recipient of our worship, and He gets to define what worship should be. You may not feel that you have a good singing voice, but that makes no difference to God. We must train our tastes and preferences so that we regard as beautiful that which God deems beautiful and holy. All of this begins in your heart.

3. Thanksgiving comes from your new heart.

Paul commanded Christians to give thanks two times in these three verses. "Be thankful," he reminded them in Colossians 3:15, and added, "giving thanks to the Lord" in verse 17. Further, we are to sing "with grace" (Col. 3:16), which is translated, "with thankfulness" in the English Standard Version.

Thanksgiving is a vital component of your heart. Without remembering to give thanks, there is a danger that you will forget that "every good and perfect gift is from above" (James 1:17). Neglecting to give thanks to God was a symptom of the wicked people in Rome (Rom. 1:25), who "did not like to retain God in their knowledge" (Rom. 1:28). By choosing this destructive path, they would be forced to face "the righteous judgment of God" (Rom. 1:32), Who would punish their evil deeds.

Take time every day to thank God. When you pray, carefully observe how much of your prayer could be classified as thanksgiving versus how much of it could be classified as requests. It is certainly right to make requests to God (Phil. 4:6), but let us not neglect to fill our hearts with thankfulness to God for all that He does for us.

A thankful, grateful heart will go far in the journey of the new you.

A CLOSER LOOK

Let's take a closer look at worship. To worship is to offer spiritual scarifies to God (1 Pet. 2:5; Heb. 13:15) in praise to Him. God has always been very specific in defining acceptable worship to His people. In the Old Testament, Nadab and Abihu failed to worship

God correctly and were killed for their unfaithfulness (Lev. 10:1-2). The sin of Cain also involved unacceptable worship (Gen. 4:1-7).

In John 4:19-24, Jesus gave four directives regarding acceptable worship for our day.

First, notice the **place** of worship. In John 4:21, Jesus said that we can worship from anywhere in the world. There was a time when Jews were required to go to a certain place, Jerusalem, to offer their sacrifices to God. Today, we can worship God wherever His people meet.

Second, Jesus discussed the **people** of worship. He said that God is seeking "true worshipers" (John 4:23), those whose hearts are seeking God's way.

Third, Jesus gave the **prescriptions** for worship. Look at John 4:24:

> God is Spirit, and those who worship Him must worship in spirit and truth.

Jesus gives an absolute – "must." Worshipers of God *must* do it a certain way. God sets the parameters for acceptable worship, and they involve the right attitudes ("in spirit") and the right authority ("in truth"). To worship "in spirit" has to do with the heart. I want to connect my spirit to God when I worship Him. To worship "in truth" means that I want to follow everything the Lord has revealed in His word regarding worship.

The Bible reveals five ways that we can acceptably express our worship to God: in song (Col. 3:16), in prayer (Acts 4:23-31), in partaking of the Lord's Supper (1 Cor. 11:23-24), in hearing the Bible read and preached (Acts 20:7), and in financial giving (1 Cor. 16:1-2).

It is important to do what God says in the way that God says to do it. This begins with ensuring your heart is full of God's word and ready to express praise to God through these prescribed avenues.

BRINGING IT ALL TOGETHER

The book of Revelation pictures Jesus standing at the door of someone's heart (Rev. 3:20). While we might generally think of the Lord knocking on the door of a non-Christian's heart, this verse is actually addressed to people who were already Christians. The Lord pleads with them to hear His voice and open the door, but He leaves the decision to them.

The only way to accomplish spiritual success is to let Jesus into your heart. Perhaps some Christians thought they opened the door when they were baptized, but, in actuality, they only cracked the door. What is the door to your heart like? Is it open for Jesus?

Opening your heart to Jesus means developing a real connection to Him. The only way to do that is by reading and studying the Bible. There is no substitute for regular Bible study and prayer.

Regular Bible study, coupled with applying what you learn from Scripture and praying to God, will only improve your relationship with God. This is how you strengthen your new heart.

QUESTIONS

1. Describe the peace of God.

2. How does the word of Christ reside in your heart?

3. Why is it important to thank God in prayer?

4. What would make worship vain or unscriptural?

5. How is spiritual success linked to your new heart?

ACTION ITEMS

1. *Write in on your heart.* Memorize Proverbs 3:5-6
2. *Count your blessings.* Make a long list of the blessings you have received. Make sure the list has at least 50 items. Keep the list handy and look over it Saturday night in preparation for worship on Sunday.

Chapter 9
A NEW HOME

ONE DAY AT A TIME

Day Fifty-Seven – Colossians 3:18-21
   1. Summarize the directions for wives.

   2. Summarize the directions for husbands.

   Prayer Starter – If you are married, pray for your spouse. If you are single and want to get married, pray for your future spouse. If you are single and do not intend to marry, then pray for families you know (mention them by name).

Day Fifty-Eight – Ephesians 5:22-33
   1. According to verse 32, about what is Paul speaking?

   2. How is a husband to love his wife?

   Prayer Starter – Thank God for the love Christ has for the church.

Day Fifty-Nine – Ephesians 6:1-4
   1. Describe the directions for children.

   2. Describe the directions for fathers.

   Prayer Starter – Pray for your parents. If your parents are deceased, thank God for them and for your memory of them. Additionally, if you are a parent, pray for your children.

Day Sixty – Matthew 19:1-9
1. How does God define marriage?

2. What is the one exception for divorce?

Prayer Starter – Pray for our culture, which continually tries to redefine marriage. Pray that God will allow people to learn His ways and follow Him before it is too late.

Day Sixty-One – 1 Peter 3:1-7
1. If a Christian woman has an unbelieving husband, what is she to do?

2. How are husbands supposed to treat their wives?

Prayer Starter – Pray for someone who is not a Christian today. Specifically name them before God.

Day Sixty-Two – Romans 7:2-3
1. How long is a wife bound by God's law to her husband?

2. If her husband dies, may she remarry?

Prayer Starter – Pray for widows and widowers.

Day Sixty-Three – Genesis 2:18-24
1. Why was woman created?

2. "Therefore a man shall _____ his father and mother and ____ _____ to his wife."

Prayer Starter – Thank God for providing for all of your needs.

WHAT'S NEW?

You are the new you everywhere you go – even in your home. In fact, the way you conduct yourself at home may be the true test of your relationship with Jesus. When you are around people with whom you are the most comfortable, do you still demonstrate your commitment to your Savior?

The good news is, the Bible gives you the blueprint for a complete home makeover. Whether you are a son or a daughter, a husband or a wife, you make a contribution to your family. Does that "at home" match the new you?

BECOMING NEW

Let's focus on three sections from the Bible that, when taken together, provide the master plan for your home makeover. We are about to begin a full renovation, from the foundation to the overall functionality and then to the focal point of the whole home.

1. The Foundation

Jesus spoke very highly of marriage and the home.

> Have you not read that He who made them at the beginning made them "male and female," and said, "For this reason a man shall leave his father and mother and be joined to his wife, and the two shall become one flesh?" So then, they are no longer two but one less. Therefore what God has joined together, let not man separate (Mat. 19:4-6).

Our Lord quoted from the Old Testament (Gen. 1:27; 2:24) and uncovered the foundation of marriage, what the whole home stands on.

First, Jesus pointed out the **people** of the home. Marriage consists of one man and one woman, because God made them "male and female." *Second,* notice the **plan** for the home: the man and the woman leave their parents' homes and create a home of their own. They are joined together by God, and become one. *Third,* the **permanent** nature of the home is described. No one is to separate what God has joined together. This relationship endures as long as they both live (Rom. 7:2-3).

The foundation of marriage is one man and one woman for life. It is inside the context of marriage – and only within marriage – that the sexual relationship is to be enjoyed (Heb. 13:4; 1 Cor. 7:2). Fornication, adultery, and divorce undermine the Scripture's teaching and crumble the home's foundation.

When your home is built on God's foundation, then you will enjoy the blessings of a "new" home.

2. The Functionality

It is important that a house is functional, isn't it? You want the floor plan to fit your lifestyle and accommodate your needs. You expect everything to work properly in your home.

God's blueprint for your new home also includes functionality. Each person has a function within the family dynamic, and God has given clear instructions with regard to that function. By focusing on each person within the home and summarizing the Bible's guidelines for them into one word, we will begin to see how the home can function at its best. Paul describes this for us:

> Wives, submit to your own husbands, as is fitting in the Lord. Husbands, love your wives and do not be bitter toward them. Children, obey your parents in all things, for this is well pleasing to the Lord. Fathers, do not provoke your children, lest they become discouraged (Col. 3:18-21).

First, wives are to **submit**. I know this isn't the most popular word, but it's the word Paul used. It means that the wife voluntarily takes the subordinate role in the home, allowing her husband to lead. This *does not* give her husband the right to mistreat her. Further, it *does not* mean she is inferior; she is not. She submits to her husband because it "is fitting in the Lord" (that is, it is the right thing to do). Woman was created to be a helper for the man (Gen. 2:18). Therefore, Paul's directive was not a social custom of his day; it is grounded in creation itself (1 Tim. 2:12-14; 1 Cor. 11:3, 8-9).

The New Testament commands all Christians – both men and women – to be active in "submitting to one another in the fear of God" (Eph. 5:21). This means both men and women must be unselfish in their thoughts and actions, being considerate of each other, and putting their needs before our own (Rom. 12:10; Phil. 2:3). That's what wives are called to do. Biblical submission is not domestic abuse. The Bible is clear that those who mistreat others will be punished in hell.

The submission Paul prescribes is an honorable position. Of the different functions in the home, the wife's role most closely resembles Jesus' earthly ministry. The Lord came to submit to His Father (John 6:38), to serve (Mark 10:45). When the wife chooses to submit to her husband in the home, she is fulfilling her God-given role.

Second, husbands are addressed. Since wives are told to submit, we might expect husbands to be commanded to lead. The Bible certainly instructs husbands to lead their families, especially providing spiritual leadership (Eph. 5:23). All throughout the Bible, men are shown as the leaders of their respective families. It is interesting, though, that Colossians 3 stresses that he lead with **love**. He is to love her "just as Christ loved the church and gave Himself for her" (Eph. 5:25). Once again, the standard is set very high. Further, he is not to "be bitter toward" her (Col. 3:19). The idea is that he is not to become abusive toward his wife. Love should govern everything he does to the point that he is willing to sacrifice for her, sympathize with her, and seek her welfare (1 Pet. 3:7).

By the way, I would also assign the word "love" to the role of fathers, who are not to discourage their children (Col. 3:21), but are to "bring them up in the training and admonition of the

Lord" (Eph. 6:4). Mothers are also taught to "love their children" (Titus 3:4).

Third, children are to **obey**. Do not overlook this. The Bible repeatedly emphasizes the correlation between disobedient children and the moral bankruptcy of a society (Rom. 1:30; 2 Tim. 3:2). Further, the Bible praises the use of parental punishment, noting that, when children grow up, they will appreciate the punishment they received (Heb. 12:9).

Children are to be obedient "in all things," another one of those phrases from which nothing is excluded. In work, play, religion, and social activities, the Lord expects children to obey their parents. Obviously, this command is to be placed within proper bounds. If a parent were to require something that is ungodly, then that child should obey God rather than men (Acts 5:29). Such circumstances would be uncommon.

Finally, observe that children are to obey their parents because "this is well pleasing to the Lord" (Col. 3:20). The new goal from chapter two continues to be the number one motivator.

The new functionality of the home will be clearly displayed when wives submit, husbands love, and children obey.

3. The Focus

Sometimes the kitchen, the dining room, or the family room will be deemed "the heart of the home." The purpose of these rooms is to bring the family together, to unite them. Likewise, the home of the new you will be focused on uniting the family toward one goal – going to heaven together.

Solomon compared children to arrows in the hand of a mighty warrior. When an arrow is shot from the bow, it is supposed to hit the target. God views children like arrows, and their target is heaven. Every parent has the responsibility to set the proper aim.

> Train up a child in the way he should go,
>   And when he is old he will not depart from it (Prov. 22:6).

Both Peter and Paul addressed Christians whose spouses were not believers. Peter wrote to women with unbelieving husbands, and said that the godly influence of the wives could win their husbands for Christ (1 Pet. 3:1-2). Similarly, Paul assured Christian women that they did not need to sever their marriages if their husbands did not believe. Instead, the Christian wives were to seek to teach their husbands how to be saved (1 Cor. 7:16).

The new you has one goal: to be in Heaven where Christ is. The family of the new you will reflect that same goal as each member of that home helps the others to follow Jesus all the way to our eternal Home.

One final note:
Marriage is for life, but it is not forever. Jesus said that there is no marriage in heaven (Mat. 22:30). The marriage relationship only lasts while both the husband and the wife live (Rom. 7:2-3). Frankly, it's weird to think that the eternal day will come when my wife, Emily, and I will no longer be husband and wife. However, that fact only accentuates the focus of our home today. If we are not preparing for eternity – together – then we'll miss the whole point. We could be married for 60 years, but if we do not help each other get to heaven, then what was the point?

Our homes here are temporary. Eternity is forever.

A CLOSER LOOK

As I drove home from work one day, a billboard along the highway caught my attention. Two rings, clearly a man's and a woman's wedding bands, stood on their sides, forming two "O's" in the word "OOPS." It was an ad for a divorce lawyer.

Does our culture's view of divorce mirror what the Bible teaches on the subject? I'll show you what the Bible teaches and then you can answer the question.

Jesus was approached by a group of men who wanted to test

Him. Their goal was to expose Him as a fraud (Matthew 19:1-12). They asked him, "Is it lawful for a man to divorce his wife for just any reason?" (Mat. 19:3). Jesus answered the question by simply stating that God's plan is for a married man and woman to remain together (Mat. 19:4-6). After all, God joined them together.

The men asked a follow-up question about the Old Testament (Mat. 19:7). When they did, they actually misrepresented the Old Testament by claiming that Moses commanded the people to divorce. Moses allowed divorce, but did not command it. The behavior of the people in Moses' day was not in accordance with God's original law on marriage (Gen. 2:24).

Jesus commanded a restoration of God's original marriage law, and answered the second question this way:

> [W]hoever divorces his wife, except for sexual immorality, and marries another commits adultery; and whoever marries her who is divorced commits adultery (Mat. 19:9).

Let's make this practical. If Mr. and Mrs. Smith are married, then God's intention is for them to remain married as long as they both live. However, if Mrs. Smith commits "sexual immorality" (or, "fornication," which means having sex with someone who is not your spouse), then Mr. Smith would have the right by God to divorce Mrs. Smith, dissolving their marriage. He is not obligated to divorce her, but he has the right from God. Since God "joined [them] together" (Mat. 19:6), only God can "un-join" them. Since Mr. Smith has the authority from God (per Mat. 19:9), then God would "un-join" the two.

If Mr. Smith, as the innocent party, wanted to remarry, he would have the option to do so (provided the woman whom he chose to marry was also Scripturally eligible). However, if Mrs. Smith (who committed fornication) wanted to remarry, she would not be permitted to do so by God because "whoever marries her who is divorced commits adultery" (Mat. 19:9). Notice the present tense verb, "commits." This means that whoever married Mrs. Smith would be committing adultery as long as they remained married.

Let's say a different couple – Mr. and Mrs. Jones – wanted to get a divorce, but neither of them had committed fornication. Perhaps their reason for the divorce was "irreconcilable differences." Could they do so and be right with God? No, because "whoever divorces his wife … and marries another commits adultery" (Mat. 19:9).

I know this is difficult to process and to accept. Floods of emotion drown this subject, making it all the more difficult to discuss. Just remember your goal – to please God. Whatever you do, please God.

BRINGING IT ALL TOGETHER

If you will follow the Bible's blueprint for a home makeover, you will experience the joys of a new home like none you have ever known. Your foundation will be rock-solid, you will function at peak levels, and your focus will guide you and your family to Heaven.

Admittedly, this will not be easy (change never is), but it will be worth it. Don't lose your perspective. Heaven is the goal. Your life should measure up to God's standard, not your own. Build your new home, and prepare for your eternal home.

QUESTIONS

1. How do husbands and fathers function as the spiritual leaders of their homes? Be specific.

2. Describe the biblical definition of submission.

3. How can a married couple repent if they learn that they do not have the scriptural right to be married?

4. If a teenager is the first New Testament Christian in his or her home, what can he or she do to influence his or her home for Christ?

5. What practical things can a family do to unite toward their goal of heaven?

ACTION ITEMS

1. *Thrive in your role.* What is one thing you can do this week to better fulfill your function in your family? How can you better lead, submit, or obey?
2. *Keep Satan out.* Assess the media that you allow into your home. Do the TV shows, Online videos, and music you consume align with the ideals of the new you? If not, do not allow them into your home.

Chapter 10
A NEW JOB

ONE DAY AT A TIME

Day Sixty-Four – Colossians 3:22-4:1

1. How does Paul say bondservants should serve their masters?

2. Who is the master of masters?

Prayer Starter – Ask God to help you interact with others in a way that will honor and please Him.

Day Sixty-Five – 1 Peter 2:18-25

1. How does Peter say servants should serve their masters?

2. "But when you ____ _____ and _____, if you take it _____ this is commendable before God."

Prayer Starter – Pray for strength to endure suffering.

Day Sixty-Six – 2 Thessalonians 3:10-16

1. If an able-bodied individual refuses to work, what does Scripture say he should not do?

2. "Work in _____ and eat _____ _____ bread."

Prayer Starter – Thank God for providing your daily bread by blessing you with the ability to pay for your needs to be met.

Day Sixty-Seven – Ephesians 6:5-9

1. When Paul writes to the Ephesians, how does he say bondservants should serve their masters?

2. "Whatever good anyone does, he will receive _____ _____ from the Lord, whether he is slave or free."

Prayer Starter – Pray that God will help you remember to serve others as though you are serving Him.

Day Sixty-Eight – 1 Timothy 6:1-5
1. Why should bondservants count their masters worthy of all honor?

2. A believing master is the bondservant's _____.

Prayer Starter – Pray that your actions will never blaspheme God and His doctrine.

Day Sixty-Nine – 1 Timothy 6:6-10
1. With what should we be content?

2. What is the danger of loving money?

Prayer Starter – Ask God to help you trust in Him instead of in material things.

Day Seventy – 1 Timothy 6:17-19
1. What are the rich commanded to do?

2. The rich should store up to lay hold on _____ _____.

Prayer Starter – Pray that God will help you to view riches as a means to serve Him.

WHAT'S NEW?

On an average work day, employed Americans (ages 25-54) spend 8.9 hours working or doing work-related activities.[1] I know people who work less than that each day, and I know people who work a lot more than that each day. It's not uncommon for a friend of mine, who is an Emergency Medical Technician to work 24 hour shifts!

The Christian experience causes us to see things from a fresh perspective – including our jobs. Students, executives, entrepreneurs, shift workers, and telecommuters all have great opportunities for Jesus in their occupations. In this chapter, we will focus on biblical principles that cast new light on your job.

> Bondservants, obey in all things your masters according to the flesh, not with eyeservice, as men-pleasers, but in sincerity of heart, fearing God. And whatever you do, do it heartily, as to the Lord and not to men, knowing that from the Lord you will receive the reward of the inheritance; for you serve the Lord Christ. But he who does wrong will be repaid for what he has done, and there is no partiality.
>
> Masters, give your bondservants what is just and fair, knowing that you also have a Master in heaven (Col. 3:22-4:1).

BECOMING NEW

The New Testament has a lot to say about slaves and masters. In fact, more is said to slaves in Colossians 3 than is said to wives, husbands, children, and fathers combined (compare Col. 3:18-21). Do not mistake slavery of New Testament times to the slavery in American history. The two were *very* different. See the *A Closer Look* section of this chapter for more information about slavery in biblical times.

---

[1] "Charts from the American Time Use Survey." U.S. Bureau of Labor Statistics. U.S. Bureau of Labor Statistics, 25 Oct. 2015. Web. 02 May 2016.

As we proceed with this chapter, I want you to think of "bondservants" as employees and "masters" as managers or employers. I am not saying they are perfect parallels, but I am saying that the principles apply.

In the last part of Colossians 3 and the first verse of Colossians 4, Paul gave several important guidelines regarding how the new you will conduct yourself in the workplace. He also provided a fresh and exciting perspective that connects your job with your faith.

1. Work with Christian integrity.

Paul offered three principles that apply to your job. *First,* Christians should honor the requests of their managers and employers at work (see the first part of verse 22). Here, Paul used almost the same phrase as he used for children toward their parents (Col. 3:21). A master "according to the flesh" is a reference to an earthly master. The point is that we should maintain our focus on our Heavenly Master – Jesus Christ – even as we submit to earthly masters.

Second, Christians are to be trustworthy at work. Some people work only when they know the boss is looking. Others only do their best work when they think a promotion or a raise may result. Paul said that we should not only do our best when people are watching, but also when people are not (thus the reference to "eyeservice" in verse 22). Further, we should labor "in sincerity of heart, fearing God," which means that our work should be free from pretense or hypocrisy.

Third, Christian employees should work as though they are actually working for the Lord. The fact is, they *do* actually work for the Lord. Your organization does not have to be a "Christian" nonprofit for you to work for Jesus there. Your school does not have to be a private, "faith-based" school for you to do the work of the Lord there. Paul said that part of doing the work of the Lord involves doing your best at your job. The new you will work "heartily as to the Lord and not to men" (Col .3:23). Christians do not steal from their jobs. This would include not taking cash or products, but it would also include not goofing off on the Internet on company time. Christians work with integrity.

2. Keep your eye on eternity.

When the Lord comes on Judgment Day (see chapter 3), you will give an account for everything you did while you lived. That includes what you did at work, too. With that in mind, Paul pointed out the eternal effects of what you do on the job.

First, there will be a **reward** for doing right at work. Paul referenced "the reward" in the middle of verse 24. The word "reward" carries with it the idea of full compensation. There may be some circumstances at work where you are cheated something that is rightfully yours as a result of a bad boss. However, on Judgment Day, you will be rewarded in full for maintaining your faith through it all. Let me be clear: this is not a physical reward, but "the reward of the inheritance" (Col. 3:24). He was talking about "the hope which is laid up for you in heaven, of which you heard before in the word of the truth of the gospel (Col. 1:5). There will be a reward.

Second, there will be **repayment** for doing wrong at work. The warning of verse 25 is chilling. Those who cast off the new you when they go to work will be repaid for what they have done. Though God loves you, and wants you to be saved (1 Tim. 2:3-4), He shows no partiality (the end of Col. 3:25). If you do wrong, He will punish you.

Third, you are urged to **remember** your Ruler. Paul said, "You serve the Lord Christ" (Col. 3:24). The word "Lord" means "master, ruler." The word "Christ" means "Messiah" and is used to signify that Jesus really is the Son of God. As a Christian, literally everything you do should be done in view of the fact that you belong to "the Lord Christ." He is your Ruler. That's a perspective you must maintain.

3. Lead with accountability.

Paul offered two principles for those who are in leadership positions at work. *First,* he said that leaders have an obligation to those they lead. Leaders at work should treat those under them in a just and fair way (Col. 4:1). There is a reciprocal duty between the employer and his or her employees. When workers meet the requirements (typically discussed in a contract or work agreement), then the boss has an obligation to fulfill his or her part of that agreement, as well. It is sinful to disrespect others and to dishonor the agreements you have made with them – even in the workplace (compare Mat. 5:37).

Second, Paul offers a realization for leaders at work. Even earthly masters have a Master in heaven (the last half of Col. 4:1). Your Heavenly Master cannot be ignored. So, lead your team at work, but do so with the awareness that your Master is aware of everything, including your motives.

A CLOSER LOOK

The slavery of the New Testament world was much different than the slavery of American history. It is believed that six million people in the Roman Empire were slaves. There were rich slaves and poor slaves; educated ones and uneducated ones. There were slaves of all races. Some slaves were victims of war, some were born into slavery, and others sold themselves into slavery in order to survive.[2]

Slaves were given opportunities to obtain special jobs and climb socially. Household slaves were the most common of all slaves. In Greco-Roman households, slaves served not only as cooks, cleaners, and personal attendants, but also as tutors for people of all ages, physicians, nurses, close companions, and managers of households. Business slaves were also common, serving both in menial jobs and in managerial positions for estates, shops, and as salesmen and contractors.[3]

This description of slavery makes it easier to understand why

---

[2] Weaver, Walton. *Truth Commentaries: Philippians and Colossians.* Bowling Green, KY: Guardian of Truth Foundation, 1996. Print. 558-561.

[3] *Ibid.,* 561.

Paul would encourage slaves to be Christian slaves instead of commanding them to be liberated from slavery (Col. 3:22-25; 1 Cor. 7:20-24).

None of this is to say that slavery was not a hard life. It all depended upon the kind of master who ruled over a slave and how a slave behaved himself or herself under the rule of the master. However, even mistreatment was not a reason for lashing back in an un-Christlike fashion. Peter said,

> Servants, be submissive to your masters with all fear, not only to the good and gentle, but also to the harsh. For this is commendable, if because of conscience toward God one endures grief, suffering wrongfully (1 Pet. 2:18-19).

It is valuable to see that the slavery of the New Testament, though not a perfect parallel to modern employee / employer relationships, provides some great regulations for Christian behavior at work.

Slavery was such a part of the New Testament culture that Paul identified as a slave of Jesus (Rom. 1:1), and said that all Christians are "slaves of righteousness" (Rom. 6:19) and "slaves of God" (Rom. 6:22).

There is one more thing I want to say about slavery in the Bible. God's word never condones mistreating someone. The Bible is clear that all humans are equal in the sight of God (Acts 10:34-35). Consequently, we should not feel that we are any better than someone else (Rom. 12:5; Phil. 2:3-4). We are to love others as we love our own selves (Mat. 22:39), treating them the way that we should be treated (Mat. 7:12).

BRINGING IT ALL TOGETHER

One night, Jesus' disciples found themselves on a boat in a terrible storm on the Sea of Galilee (Mat. 14:22-33). Jesus had not gone with them in the boat, but He came to them later, miraculously walking on the sea. When His disciples first saw Him, they were scared to death. They cried out for fear, saying, "It's a ghost!" But

Jesus calmed them, assuring them of His presence.

Peter, always the outspoken one, said, "Lord, if it is you, command me to come to You on the water." Jesus said, "Come." Peter stepped out of the boat and onto the water with His eyes on Jesus. That must have been an incredible moment. I do not know how long Peter stood on the water, nor how many steps he took, but I know that "when he saw that the wind was boisterous, he was afraid; and beginning to sink he cried out, saying, 'Lord, save me!'" (Mat. 19:30). Jesus stretched out His hand to Peter, and got him back in the boat.

Peter messed up when he took his eyes off of Jesus. He began to focus on his insecurity caused by the wind and the storms rather than the safety that Jesus could provide him.

The same will happen to you if you lose your focus on Jesus. At work, this may involve giving in to the temptation to gossip with coworkers or to pretend to be busy rather than actually working. It could involve cheating, dishonesty, or badmouthing another employee so you will get the raise instead of them. From a leadership perspective, losing your focus on Jesus could come in the form of mistreating those who report to you, or blaming your team for a mistake that was your responsibility.

I am certainly not saying that it is wrong to participate in a competitive work environment. However, it is never right to cast off your faith – even for the sake of an extra dollar.

Imagine the influence you will have for Jesus when the new you shows up to work! It may take some time, but people will notice the difference. Glorify God in it.

QUESTIONS

1. Explain the differences between the slavery in the New Testament world and the slavery of American history.

2. Why would it be morally wrong to waste time on Facebook while you are on the clock at work?

3. What should they do if their work has a strict "no proselytizing" policy?

4. How can a leader in the workplace model Christianity at work?

5. How can an employee model Christianity at work?

ACTION ITEMS

1. *Cut the complaints.* Don't participate in complaining at work (be it about your job or about your manager or boss). Your coworkers are likely to notice the difference!
2. *Work with integrity.* Assess your habits at work to determine if change is warranted. Work like you work for the Lord!

Chapter 11
A NEW MISSION

ONE DAY AT A TIME

Day Seventy-One – Colossians 4:2-6

1. For what did Paul want them to pray?

2. Why should we speak with grace, seasoned with salt?

Prayer Starter – Pray that God will give you opportunities to spread His saving message with someone.

Day Seventy-Two – Matthew 28:18-20

1. "Go … and _____ _____ of all the nations."

2. What were they to be taught to do?

Prayer Starter – Thank God for the good news of Jesus and for its availability to all nations.

Day Seventy-Three – Mark 16:9-16

1. How does this reading differ from what you read yesterday (which records the same command)?

2. Why did Jesus mention belief twice, but baptism only once?

Prayer Starter – Pray that your influence will glorify God.

Day Seventy-Four – 1 Peter 3:15-17

1. What should we already be ready to do?

2. Is all suffering bad?

Prayer Starter – Thank God for allowing you to be His servant.

Day Seventy-Five – Hebrews 5:12-14
1. Why were these Christians reprimanded?

2. What was the solution to their problem?

Prayer Starter – Pray that you will be spiritually strong by growing in your knowledge of the word.

Day Seventy-Six – Romans 10:11-15
1. What is a Christian's role in helping a non-Christian?

2. "How shall they hear without a _____?"

Prayer Starter – Pray for people who are lost in sin, that their hearts will turn to the truth. Be specific in naming people you know who need to obey the gospel.

Day Seventy-Seven – Luke 24:46-49
1. Why did Jesus say it was necessary for Him to die and rise from the dead on the third day?

2. To whom was this saving message to be preached?

Prayer Starter – Thank God for the sacrifice of Jesus on the cross, and for the effects of that sacrifice on your life.

WHAT'S NEW?

The word "evangelize" means to spread the good news, the "gospel." Paul was always "ready to preach the gospel" to anyone who would listen (Rom. 1:15).

Sharing the message of Jesus is a privilege in which every Christian can (and should) participate. In fact, Jesus commands His disciples to tell others of Him. This is often called the "Great Commission."

> Go therefore and make disciples of all the nations, baptizing them in the name of the Father and of the Son and of the Holy Spirit, teaching them to observe all things that I have commanded you; and lo, I am with you always, even to the end of the age." Amen (Mat. 28:19-20).

This is the mission of the new you: to teach the truth to as many people as possible so that their souls might be saved.

Paul constantly searched for individuals whom he could tell about Jesus. In this lesson's text, Paul gives three things Christians can do to fulfill their mission.

> Continue earnestly in prayer, being vigilant in it with thanksgiving; meanwhile praying also for us, that God would open to us a door for the word, to speak the mystery of Christ, for which I am also in chains, that I may make it manifest, as I ought to speak.
> Walk in wisdom toward those who are outside, redeeming the time. Let your speech always be with grace, seasoned with salt, that you may know how you ought to answer each one (Col. 4:2-6).

BECOMING NEW

1. Open your eyes.
Paul asked His brothers and sisters in Christ to pray for him,

especially that he would have opportunities to share the gospel. Notice two key points from what he said in verse 3. *First,* Paul asked them to pray that God would "open ... a door for the word." In a world that is becoming increasingly hostile to the Bible, the temptation is to only seek to share the gospel when someone asks you to do so. Paul's response to that would be,

> How then shall they call on Him in whom they have not believed? And how shall they believe in Him of whom they have not heard? And how shall they hear without a preacher? (Rom. 10:14).

Paul would seek out people with whom he could share the gospel, even to the point of asking God to providentially place him in situations in which he could evangelize.

Second, Paul wanted to let the word speak. When opportunities arose, Paul would not give people his opinions about spiritual matters, he would let the word speak (Col. 4:3). This is in accordance with what Jesus commanded when He said to "preach the gospel to every creature" (Mark 16:15). Though Paul was "in chains" (in prison – because of his preaching!), he would not be made to stop speaking God's word. He said, "I ought to speak [the word]" (Col. 4:4; 1 Cor. 9:16).

Now that you are a Christian, you have the same privilege and obligation to spread the saving message of Jesus to everyone. Keep a sharp eye out for the opened doors that God gives you. It might be a family member or a close friend; it could be a coworker or a new acquaintance – whatever the case, preach Jesus to them!

2. Walk the walk.

Paul said, "Walk in wisdom toward those who are outside" (Col. 4:5). The outsiders are those who are outside of Christ, that is, they are not Christians (compare 1 The. 4:12; 1 Tim. 3:7). "Wisdom" is applied knowledge, specifically a knowledge of God's will (Col. 1:9-10). The reason you are to walk with wisdom is because those outside of Christ are watching you. They want to know if you really believe the things that you profess. By living your convictions, you are letting your light shine (Mat. 5:16). You want to live in a way that will not cause others to have a negative impression of the Lord or His church. In other words, walk the walk. Doing so will create evangelistic opportunities.

Additionally, you should "redeem the time." A simple definition of the word "redeem" would be "to rescue from loss." Imagine you are at the park on a hot summer day. The ice cream man comes by, and you decide to indulge. About the time you pull out your cash, a strong gust of wind comes through, blowing the money from your hand, into the nearby creek. You rush downstream from where the bills landed so you can frantically grab them from the flow. You are "redeeming" the money, rescuing it from loss.

Paul said that you must redeem your time. Time is precious; it is limited, it is fleeting, and we are not promised another second of it (James 4:13-17). Since Paul has been discussing evangelism throughout this section, it is reasonable to conclude that to "redeem the time" is to use every evangelistic opportunity you are given, trying your best not to let any slip through the cracks.

3. Talk the talk.

Carefully construct the words you say in order to cultivate opportunities to share the gospel. Paul offered two ways to accomplish this in Colossians 4:6.

First, Paul said to speak with grace (Col. 4:6). Notice that your speech should "always be with grace," indicating that both private and public conversations should be gracious. Just as salt improves the taste of food, your speech should be flavored with good things to improve the conversation around you.

Second, Paul said to be prepared: "that you may know how you ought to answer each one" (Col. 4:6). The implication is that some people will ask you questions about being a Christian.

This is a great opportunity to tell them about Jesus! Here's how Peter phrased it:

> But sanctify the Lord God in your hearts, and always be ready to give a defense to everyone who asks you a reason for the hope that is in you, with meekness and fear (1 Pet. 3:15).

Do not wait for these opportunities to come to you. Jesus said to "go" and preach (Mat. 28:19). Go to those who need a relationship with Jesus. Go to those who are not doing what the New Testament teaches they must do to be saved. Cultivate opportunities for the Lord by opening your eyes, walking the walk, and talking the talk.

A CLOSER LOOK

Christians have been working to execute their mission since the church began. The church that Christ built was established on the Day of Pentecost following Christ's crucifixion, resurrection, and ascension. You can read about its beginning in Acts chapter 2, when three thousand souls were baptized (Acts 2:38, 41) and added by the Lord to His church (Acts 2:47). The church to which they were added was the one Jesus had previously promised to build (Mat. 16:18). This is the "one body" about which Paul spoke (Eph. 4:4; 1:22-23).

Those new Christians immediately began teaching others. Before long, "the number of men came to be about five thousand" (Acts 4:4). A little later, "believers were increasingly added to the Lord, multitudes of both men and women" (Acts 5:14). The number of disciples was multiplying (Acts 6:1) as "the word of God spread" (Acts 6:7).

They spread that saving message with enthusiasm and passion. They knew that Jesus is the only way to get to Heaven (John 14:6; Mat. 7:13-14, 21-23). Even when "a great persecution arose against the church" (Acts 8:1), they would not abandon their God-given mission. At one point, the Christians in Jerusalem were so persecuted that they were made to leave their homes and their city. However, "those who were scattered went everywhere preaching the word" (Acts 8:4). It is interesting to note that everyone was scattered "except the apostles" (Acts 8:1). Evangelism is not just something that "the preacher" is supposed to do; it is something you are supposed to do!

Christians in the New Testament took their mission seriously, owning up to their personal responsibility. As a result, "the churches were strengthened in the faith, and increased in number daily" (Acts 16:5). Rather than making excuses (such as, "How can we possibly take the gospel to the whole world?!" or "No one is interested in hearing the gospel today"), they diligently worked for the Lord. God blessed their work. When Paul wrote to the Colossians, he was able to say that "the gospel has come to you, as it has also in all the world" (Col. 1:5-6). Further, he declared that the gospel "was preached to every creature under heaven" (Col. 1:23).

In an age of social media, viral videos, GPS, automobiles, and airplanes, what excuse do we have for failing to share Jesus with others? I believe God has blessed us with each of these mediums so that we can use them to fulfill our mission.

BRINGING IT ALL TOGETHER

Take another look at the *Tell Me About Your Baptism* section. How did you feel when you learned what the Lord wanted you to do to be saved? Think about the urgency that you felt to obey God in baptism once you knew that it was required in order for you to be right with God.

Now think about all of the lost souls who need that same saving message. How will they learn of Jesus and His great sacrifice on the cross? Who will tell them?

> For whoever calls on the name of the LORD shall be saved."
> How then shall they call on Him in whom they have not believed?
> And how shall they believe in Him of whom they have not heard?
> And how shall they hear without a preacher? (Rom. 10:14-15)

You – the new you – are God's plan for lost people to come to know Jesus. Unless you tell them, they may never know the truth.

Your message is good news! However, some, unwilling to conform to God's standard for their lives, will reject it. When that happens (and it will … a lot), pray for them and keep trying to share the gospel with them. Ultimately, though, you should remember that it is God's word that has the power to save souls (Rom. 1:16; Heb. 4:12; 2 Tim. 3:16-17), not your ability. Do the best you can to share that message, then leave it up to their hearts to accept it or reject it.

If one soul responds to Jesus in baptism and to live the life of the new you, then everything you have done is worth it.

Go. Spread the truth with urgency, joy, and love. Fulfill the mission of the new you.

QUESTIONS

1. What are the consequences of neglecting the Great Commission?

2. Why is it important to emphasize that the Bible only speaks of one church?

3. How does "walking the walk" and "talking the talk" lead to evangelistic opportunities?

4. What was the key to the swift growth of the New Testament church in the book of Acts?

5. How can you "redeem the time" for future evangelistic opportunities?

ACTION ITEMS

1. *A worldwide audience.* Use your social media account(s) to spread the gospel. This could be as simple as writing something yourself or sharing a post that was originally shared on your congregation's page (like a sermon video or a Bible graphic).
2. *Be ready always.* With the help of another Christian, develop an outline that you can use to teach the gospel to someone.
3. *Go into your world.* List five people you know who need the gospel.

   _____
   _____
   _____
   _____
   _____

   Pray for these people for one week. Next week, ask them to discuss the Bible with you. Invite another Christian to help you.

Chapter 12
A NEW COMMUNITY

ONE DAY AT A TIME

Day Seventy-Eight – Colossians 4:7-15
   1. What made Tychicus a good friend?

   2. How was Epaphras a good friend?

Prayer Starter – Thank God for the support you have received from your Christian friends.

Day Seventy-Nine – Proverbs 12:26; 13:20; 22:24-25
   1. Describe the spiritual value of positive friends.

   2. What is the risk of befriending bad influences?

Prayer Starter – Pray for wisdom in choosing your friendships.

Day Eighty – John 15:11-15
   1. How has Jesus demonstrated His desire to be your friend?

   2. What must you do to be His friend?

Prayer Starter – Thank God for the privilege of having a friendship with Jesus.

Day Eighty-One – Proverbs 27:1-27
   1. What does this passage say about friends?

   2. How are a friend's wounds "faithful"?

Prayer Starter – Thank God for friends who correct you and help you to be a better Christian.

Day Eighty-Two – Proverbs 17:17; 18:24; Ephesians 5:11; James 4:4

1. If one wishes to have friends, what must he or she do?

2. What effect does befriending the world have on your relationship with God?

Prayer Starter – Thank God for your friends. Mention them by name to Him.

Day Eighty-Three – Romans 12:9-15

1. How will non-hypocritical love look?

2. What principles for relationships are given that you could apply to your friendships?

Prayer Starter – Pray for humility, that God will help your heart to rejoice when others rejoice.

Day Eighty-Four – 2 Corinthians 6:14-18

1. Why cannot Christians have fellowship with (participate in) lawlessness and darkness?

2. How are Christians to conduct themselves in relation to sin?

Prayer Starter – Pray that God will help you to be holy in this unholy world.

WHAT'S NEW?

Other than Bible study and prayer, there is probably no better way for you to grow as the new you than to surround yourself with Christian friends. Your Christian community can offer something to your faith that no one else can offer – empathy. They get it. They know what it is like to work to transform into the new you. They know the struggles of fighting off temptation, and they know what it's like to mess up from time to time. They can appreciate the effort you make to "walk the walk and talk the talk." They share in the new mission of taking the gospel to everyone.

Paul understood the value of the Christian community. As he closed the book of Colossians, he mentioned some of his closest companions.

> Tychicus, a beloved brother, faithful minister, and fellow servant in the Lord, will tell you all the news about me. I am sending him to you for this very purpose, that he may know your circumstances and comfort your hearts, with Onesimus, a faithful and beloved brother, who is one of you. They will make known to you all things which are happening here.
> Aristarchus my fellow prisoner greets you, with Mark the cousin of Barnabas (about whom you received instructions: if he comes to you, welcome him), and Jesus who is called Justus. These are my only fellow workers for the kingdom of God who are of the circumcision; they have proved to be a comfort to me.
> Epaphras, who is one of you, a bondservant of Christ, greets you, always laboring fervently for you in prayers, that you may stand perfect and complete in all the will of God. For I bear him witness that he has a great zeal for you, and those who are in Laodicea, and those in Hierapolis. Luke the beloved physician and Demas greet you. Greet the brethren who are in Laodicea, and Nymphas and the church that is in his house (Col. 4:7-15).

BECOMING NEW

Paul was writing the book of Colossians while he was under house arrest for preaching the gospel. In those days, associating with Paul may have won you more enemies than friends. Yet, the men whom Paul mentioned here stood by him through it all. From them, we can learn three great lessons about the value of our Christian community.

1. Your new community supports you.

Tychicus was a great support to Paul. The apostle calls him his "faithful minister and fellow servant in the Lord" (Col. 4:7). "Minister" means servant and "faithful" means trustworthy, dependable. Tychicus ministered *to* Paul and *for* Paul. Further, he was a "fellow servant." That phrase literally means, "co-slave," or a servant of the same Master.

The friendship between Paul and Tychicus beautifully illustrates the value of Christian support. Tychicus was willing to stay with Paul even though Paul's situation was difficult. Your Christian friends will stand with you, too, when you endure difficulties.

Onesimus is also mentioned. He and Paul met when Onesimus was a runaway slave. Paul shared the gospel with him, and encouraged him to return to his master, Philemon, to make things right. We read a letter Paul wrote regarding Onesimus in the book of Philemon in the New Testament. Onesimus was a new man after his baptism. He was "a faithful and beloved brother" (Col. 4:9), and apparently also a native of Colossae. Onesimus would bring the Colossians up to date on Paul's work.

Aristarchus is called a "fellow prisoner." It seems that Aristarchus, along with some others, took turns visiting Paul while he was imprisoned (compare Mat. 25:36).

Mark, Barnabas's cousin (Col. 4:10) and Jesus, who is also called Justus (Jesus was a fairly common name back then) are also mentioned as being Paul's "only fellow workers for the kingdom of God" who were of Jewish decent (Col. 4:11).

Paul was a Hebrew (Phil. 3:5), but it seems that most of his countrymen had turned against him. In fact, the Jews – his own people – wanted to kill him from the moment he became a Christian (Acts 9:23). It is no wonder Paul said Mark and Justus "proved to be a comfort" to him. They all stood together, united in Christ.

Your new community will do the same for you. They understand that the spiritual work in which you are involved is *real* and *worthwhile*. It is *important*. Your Christian friends will support you in it, just as you will want to support them as they work for the Lord.

2. Your new community prays for you.

Epaphras was a great friend. It seems that he was the first person to preach the gospel to the ancient city of Colossae (Col. 1:7), and he had given Paul a report about the work of the church there (Col. 1:8-9). Paul said that Epaphras was "always laboring fervently for [them] in prayers" (Col. 4:12). The word "laboring" indicates that he struggled and agonized for them in his prayers. He had a genuine interest in their spiritual welfare.

Epaphras prayed that the Christians in Colossae would "stand perfect and complete in all the will of God" (Col. 4:12). He wanted them to continue to mature as Christians and to stand firm in their convictions from God's word.

The Bible says that "[t]he prayer of a righteous person has great power as it is working" (James 5:16, ESV). Tremendous good can come from Christian friends praying for each other.

Please know that I am praying for you in your journey of the new you. I hope you will pray for me.

3. You new community cares about you.

Paul also said that Epaphras had "a great zeal" for the church in Colossae (Col. 4:13). The English Standard Version says Epaphras "worked hard for you." In other words, he truly cared about them. He was willing to do whatever needed be done to spiritually help them.

You have people like that in your life, too, whether you realize it or not. The elders of the congregation where you worship watch over your soul, and genuinely care about you, much like Epaphras cared for the Colossians. Your preacher cares about you; he preaches week in and week out because he cares for your soul. These are only a few of many examples.

Paul also mentioned Luke and Demas (Col. 4:14), who sent their greetings to the church in Colossae. It means a lot when Christian friends can keep in touch, though they live far apart from each other. One of my best friends lives over 600 miles, around 10 hours driving time, from me. Thanks to the phone and the Internet, we can continue to enjoy the blessings of Christian friendship.

A CLOSER LOOK

The Bible says a lot about the value of godly friendships. As a steel knife is sharpened by another piece of steel, so a friend can use words and actions to positively influence another friend (Prov. 27:17). On the other side of that thought, there is this warning:

> Do not be deceived: "Evil company corrupts good habits" (1 Cor. 15:33).

Just as a positive influence can be spiritually helpful, a negative influence can be spiritually detrimental. For example, look at Proverbs 22:24-25:

> Make no friendship with an angry man,
>   And with a furious man do not go,
> Lest you learn his ways
>   And set a snare for your soul.

Since befriending worldliness is positioning yourself at odds with God (James 4:4), you must carefully choose those whom you allow to influence you.

Christian friends remind us that we are not alone in our faith. Satan wants you to feel alone. He will tempt you to isolate yourself from other Christians. Do not let him! In the past, he has been successful at convincing God's people to give up because they felt alone (Elijah gave in to this, 1 Kings 19:10, 14). However, our Christian community reminds us that we are *not* alone. We can "contend earnestly for the faith" (Jude 3) together.

BRINGING IT ALL TOGETHER

As you continue to grow as a Christian, you may feel your relationships with your non-Christian friends begin to drift apart. That's because you have different values and goals now. You probably do not do some of the things that you and your friends used to do. Perhaps you don't use the same language they use. This kind of drift is natural. Honestly, it's the way it should be.

You are now a citizen of Heaven (Phil. 3:20), a member of God's family (1 Tim. 3:15), a soldier in His army (Eph. 6:10-20). You are a member of the church that belongs to Christ (Acts 2:47), which is a holy nation of God's own possession (1 Pet. 2:9). You are walking in the light (1 John 1:7). You are different now; you're new. "For what fellowship has righteousness with lawlessness? And what communion has light with darkness?" (2 Cor. 6:14). You are called to be holy (1 Pet. 1:15-16). Others, who have not answered the gospel's call, will not share those goals.

I'm not saying that you should not have friends who are not Christians. You definitely *should!* They are your greatest prospects for your new mission of spreading the gospel. Continue to let them know that you value your friendship with them, but also stress that you are different. Find a way to share the gospel with them and invite them to come with you to a worship service. Be ready to answer the questions they may have. In doing so, your non-Christian friends just might become your Christian friends!

Just be sure that you surround yourself with people who will support you, care about you, and pray for you in your Christianity. You need that support from them, and they need support from you.

QUESTIONS

1. How has your new community supported you through your new you journey?

2. Why is it spiritually dangerous for a Christian to isolate himself or herself?

3. How does faithful worship attendance help us to connect with our brothers and sisters?

4. List ten applications you can make from Proverbs 27.

5. How can a Christian carefully walk the tightrope of living in the world, but not participating in worldliness or sinfulness?

ACTION ITEMS

1. *Reach out.* Initiate a time to get together with Christian friends this week outside of a worship service.
2. *Go into your world, part 2.* Following up from last week's actions items, invite the people for whom you have been praying to study the Bible with you and another Christian this week.

Chapter 13
FOREVER NEW

ONE DAY AT A TIME

Day Eighty-Five – John 14:1-6
 1. What is "the place" Jesus promised to prepare?

 2. For whom did Jesus say He was going to prepare a place?

 Prayer Starter – Thank God for the promise of heaven.

Day Eighty-Six – Revelation 21:1-4
 1. How is Heaven described in these verses?

 2. List the things that will not be in heaven.

 Prayer Starter – Spend some time daydreaming about Heaven. Then, tell God exactly why you want to go there.

Day Eighty-Seven – Revelation 21:22-27
 1. Why is there no sun or moon in heaven?

 2. What will "by no means enter it"?

 Prayer Starter – Thank God for His promise that you can be in His presence eternally in heaven.

Day Eighty-Eight – 2 Timothy 4:1-8
 1. What reward did Paul say he would receive for his faithfulness?

 2. Who else will receive that reward?

 Prayer Starter – Pray that God will give you the strength to remain faithful throughout your life.

Day Eighty-Nine – 1 Corinthians 15:50-58

1. "_____ is swallowed up in victory."

2. What should Christians do in response to this victory?

Prayer Starter – Thank God for the assurance that your service to Him is not in vain.

Day Ninety – John 5:25-30

1. Will everyone who has died be resurrected?

2. How will the resurrected people be separated? To what will they be resurrected?

Prayer Starter – Pray for those who are not prepared for the resurrection.

Bonus Day – Matthew 25:31-46

1. Who had the righteous "sheep" served?

2. How long will punishment last? How long will the reward of "life" last?

Prayer Starter – Pray that, on Judgment Day, you will be found by God to be a good and faithful servant.

WHAT'S NEW?

You – the new you – are here for a very specific purpose: to bring glory to God by obeying His will (Eccl. 12:13-14; Rev. 4:11). You became the new you when you obeyed the gospel through your baptism for the forgiveness of your sins. The new has come to stay in your life (2 Cor. 5:17, see chapter 1) as you work to conform to your new standard, to fight your new enemy, and to grow closer to Jesus.

God wants you to be *forever new*. The disappointing part about *physical* new things is that the newness eventually wears off. Being *spiritually* new, however, does not lose its luster! The truly amazing thing about the new you is this: the more you grow as a Christian and the more you know about Christ, the newer your life will become. The more you learn about and experience God's love, the newer it seems. It gets more beautiful, more meaningful, and even more unfathomable.

Here is the best part: as deep and rich and limitless as your relationship with God can become while you are alive, nothing can compare to the newness that you will know in Heaven.

BECOMING NEW

1. Heaven's nature will be new.

Heaven is described as a "new heaven and a new earth" four times in Scripture. When John was permitted to see a vision of this magnificent place, he said that he "saw a new heaven and a new earth, for the first heaven and earth had passed away. Also there was no more sea" (Rev. 21:1). This description indicates that the very nature of Heaven will be new. It will not be on this earth or even in the physical realm. Heaven is a spiritual place. Jesus was clear that He would "go" to prepare heaven for His people (John 14:1-6). Further, He said that if we store up treasures on earth, we will miss Heaven (Mat. 6:19-21). These descriptions also make it clear that heaven will not be on earth.

Heaven is "new" in the sense that it will contain a new happiness; it is a place so full of joy that we cannot even begin to imagine it here (Isa. 65:17-19). It will also be a place of worship (Isa. 66:22-23). You may think, "We worship here, so how is a place of worship new?". Just imagine worshiping in the very presence of God (Rev. 21:1-4); literally seeing Him on His throne as you offer your praise to His worthy name. That will be an amazing – and new – experience.

Heaven will be filled with the righteous (2 Pet. 3:13). Contrast that with the massive amounts of evil that reside in this world, and you can appreciate – and long for – the newness of dwelling in a place "in which righteousness dwells" (2 Pet. 3:13).

Heaven – by its very nature – will be new!

2. Heaven's residents will be new.

Yes, Heaven will be inhabited by the new you, but you will be new in more ways than one. Not only will you be "new" in the sense that Christ recreated you to be new in baptism, you will also be new in your very essence. Paul said "we shall all be changed" (1 Cor. 15:51). When he said that, he was talking about our nature. We will not be flesh and blood in heaven. We will go from corruptible to incorruptible, from dishonor to glory, from weakness to power, from a natural body to a spiritual body (1 Cor. 15:42-44). Notice that word "incorruptible." While we do not know how that incorruptible body will look (1 John 3:2), it is clear that this incorruptibility will alleviate all of the burdens that are associated with a perishable body.

While you will be made new, the Bible emphasizes that you will retain your identity. Even in Heaven, you will be you. Your memories of life on Earth will remain. You will know all of your acquaintances who are there with you (though your relationships with them – such as your spouse or your children – will be different there [see chapter 9]). This information is based on the account of the rich man and Lazarus told by Jesus in Luke 16:19-31. Jesus said that, after both men died, they retained their personal identities and memories. They knew each other and the rich man remembered his brothers who were still alive.

In Heaven, you will still be you, yet you will be in a new place and you will have been made new.

3. Heaven's song will be new.

In the book of Revelation, John noticed a new song that was sung in Heaven (Rev. 14:3). When he heard the new song in Revelation 5, he noted that it was a song of victory (Rev. 5:9-10, 12).

I cannot think of anything more appropriate to do in Heaven than to praise God in song for the victory that He has allowed us to enjoy.

> So when this corruptible has put on incorruption, and this mortal has put on immortality, then shall be brought to pass the saying that is written: "Death is swallowed up in victory" (1 Cor. 15:54).

Can you imagine how the singing will sound in Heaven? Take a minute to daydream about that. I imagine we will sing enthusiastically, joyfully, gratefully, and at the top of our lungs (if we were to have lungs in our incorruptible bodies). Think about the great privilege of getting to sing that song. *That song* will be unlike any song you will ever sing in a worship service here. It will be the song of a realized hope, the song of faith becoming sight, the song of *victory!*

Not everyone will get to sing the victory song. I don't like to think about it, but it's just true: not everyone will go to Heaven. Jesus said,

> Not everyone who says to Me, 'Lord, Lord,' shall enter the kingdom of heaven, but he who does the will of My Father in heaven (Mat. 7:21).

That verse further speaks to the necessity of our mission.

It also should remind you that you must not give up. Look long and hard at these words — **_Heaven will be worth it._** Every battle you have ever fought against sin, every time someone made fun of you, every feeling of loneliness or discouragement – endure it all because Heaven will be worth it!

Please do not miss singing that new song in your new body in that new and wonderful place. Don't miss being in the presence of Almighty God. After all He has done to make you the new you, please don't miss seeing Jesus.

Don't miss Heaven!

A CLOSER LOOK

In addition to what *will* be in heaven, the Bible also tells us some things that *will not* be there.

1. There will be no more separation.

Death, which causes a separation for a time, will be no more (Rev. 21:4). It is hard to even imagine a life free from death. Heaven is called "everlasting" or "eternal" life (John 3:16; Titus 1:2). We will go there, and "thus we shall always be with the Lord" (1 The. 4:17).

2. There will be no more sin.

John noted,

> But there shall by no means enter it anything that defiles, or causes an abomination or a lie, but only those who are written in the Lamb's Book of Life (Rev. 21:27).

Your name was written in the Lamb's Book of Life when you were baptized into Christ (Phil. 4:3; Rev. 3:5). Think about that – *your name* is written in heaven! You have a reservation (1 Pet. 1:4)!

Think about what it means that there will be no more sin; we will not have to be concerned with falling into temptation! You will be right where you belong – safe with God.

3. There will be no more sorrow.

Heaven is the place where we will never grow old. If you have ever had your heart torn apart in the death of a loved one, then you can appreciate the incorruptible nature of heaven's residents. There will be no more wrinkles, scars, disabilities, aging, aches, pains, injuries, and illnesses! "[T]he former things have passed away" (Rev. 21:4)! All of the sadness we experienced in this life will be no more!

*****

It's no wonder that John ended the Revelation by saying, "Even so, come, Lord Jesus!" (Rev. 22:20). Having seen visions of this amazing place, John could not wait to get there with all of his brothers and sisters in Christ.

BRINGING IT ALL TOGETHER

Heaven is *real!* Jesus said it is real (John 14:2-3), and God, who cannot lie, has promised it to the faithful (Titus 1:2). Paul was convinced that everyone who loves the Lord will know heaven's rewards when the Judgment Day comes (2 Tim. 4:8).

Heaven is for *you!* Can you believe it?! During His earthly ministry, Jesus gave a picture of the Judgment Day. As He welcomed the faithful into heaven, He said, "Come, you blessed of My Father, inherit the kingdom **prepared for you** from the foundation of the world" (Mat. 25:34, emphasis added).

Please, dear Christian, don't miss heaven. This book has been a humble effort to equip you to live the life of the new you. However, as I stated at the beginning, this is not just about this life. It's about your goal – being with Jesus Christ in heaven – and it's about helping as many people as possible to get there, too – your family, your friends, your coworkers, and anyone else with whom you can share the gospel!

Satan will do everything he can to distract your focus, but "He who is in you is greater than he who is in the world" (1 John 4:4). You can overcome! Paul said,

> For I am persuaded that neither death nor life, nor angels nor principalities nor powers, nor things present nor things to come, nor height nor depth, nor any other created thing, shall be able to separate us from the love of God which is in Christ Jesus our Lord (Rom. 8:38-39).

The last day on earth will come, marking the sunrise of the eternal day. The Lord will come in the clouds and take us home to heaven, right where we belong. We will worship Him, thank Him, and praise Him as we stand, side-by-side, with God's people from every age.

That day is coming! When it comes, I can't wait to sing the song of victory with you – *the new you.*

QUESTIONS

1. How does the journey of the new you continue through eternity in heaven?

2. Why will some people not be permitted into heaven, even though they were religious people?

3. How do you know heaven is real?

4. Is it biblically acceptable to be confident that you are going to heaven?

5. Why is heaven described as "a new heaven and a new earth"?

ACTION ITEMS

1. *Finally free!* Make a list of the things that you are glad will NOT be in heaven (e.g., cancer).
2. *Sing to me of heaven.* Get a song book from the church building, and look up five songs about heaven (most songs books have a topical index in the back, which groups songs together under a given topic). Read through the words of those songs to increase your appreciation for heaven. As you do, write down phrases in the songs that you may not understand. Ask a song leader for clarification on those phrases.

    While songs are not inspired by God (as the Bible is), they can express biblical truths in ways that can help us to better appreciate the teachings of truth.

ACKNOWLEDGMENTS

The existence of this volume must be attributed, first of all, to God's goodness toward me. It is my humble prayer that this book glorifies Him, and helps others to glorify Him.

Second, I must acknowledge my gracious family and friends, who have helped me overcome my own insecurities about writing a book. They have offered great advice which has vastly improved the final product.

Special thanks to my wife, **Emily Hatfield**, to whom this book is dedicated. She has been a valued sounding board since this was only a faint idea. Her help is woven into every part of this publication – from the grammar and sentence structure to the *Action Items* at the end of each chapter to the layout and design. God's blessings come to me through Emily every single day (Prov. 19:14). *I love you — A & F!*

Paul Sain has been an encourager to me for virtually my whole life. He and I have been brainstorming and daydreaming together for around 15 years. It was an honor to work alongside him in the pulpit for 7 years, and our collaborative efforts continue to bless my life. Thank you, Paul, for putting up with all of my "rookie" questions throughout this publishing process, and thank you for believing in me and this volume. I look forward to many more conversations that begin with, *"I've been thinking."*

I do not think I could do my job as a preacher of the gospel without the encouragement and friendship of **Brad McNutt**. Brad first saw the material that would become this book in October 2014. Since then, he has helped me to fine tune the chapter headings and clarify the arguments presented here. He has picked me up when I began to doubt whether I could do it.

Michael Whitworth was probably the first person to ~~push~~ *encourage* me to write. To say that Michael has been generous in sharing his knowledge and research would be an understatement. His kindness and encouragement are complimented by his humor. If you are Michael's Facebook friend, then you know that he is not all work and no play. Thanks, Michael, for your generosity, encouragement, work, and your treasured friendship.

Gary and Christy Jenkins are continual encouragers. My appreciation for their prayers, support, and friendship cannot be adequately expressed.

I will forever be indebted to **Jessica Donnovant**, **Molly Ferrie**, and **Brandon Grieves** for editing the manuscript. They had the unenviable job of trying to make me sound good. These three Christians willingly gave of themselves to help make this work a reality. Thank you!

Thanks to the **North Charleston church of Christ**, whom it is my privilege to serve in the pulpit. They love the truth, and have encouraged me as some of the material in this book was presented in messages.

Special thanks to **Brian Glasshof** and **Richard Hopkins**, the shepherds under whom I serve at North Charleston, who were kind enough to allow me time away from the pulpit in order to write, and who have encouraged me throughout this process. It is a privilege to serve the Lord under their guidance.

Finally, **thank you** for reading this book. *To God be the glory!*

ABOUT THE AUTHOR

Robert Hatfield preaches for the North Charleston church of Christ in Charleston, South Carolina. He is married to Emily, and they have one daughter. Robert became a Christian on March 23, 1998.

Robert studied Mass Media and Bible at Freed-Hardeman University, from which he graduated in May 2010. Prior to moving to South Carolina, he preached for seven years in Tennessee. Robert is the founder and director of The Light Network (www.thelightnetwork.tv), a Christian podcast network that empowers people for daily Christian living. He hosts several podcasts including *Preachers in Training*, *Late Night at TLN*, and *The New You*.

The Light Network
www.thelightnetwork.tv

Christian podcasts that will encourage your soul, enlighten your mind, and empower your faith.

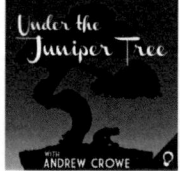

GET IT ON Google Play

Listen on Apple Podcasts

Google Play and the Google Play logo are trademarks of Google Inc.
Apple Podcasts and the Apple Podcasts logo are trademarks of Apple Inc.

THE NEW YOU PODCAST
DAILY BIBLICAL GUIDANCE FOR YOUR CHRISTIAN LIFE.

HOSTED BY ROBERT HATFIELD

- Listen online at **TheLightNetwork.tv**
- GET IT ON **Google Play**
- Listen on **Apple Podcasts**

The Light Network
www.thelightnetwork.tv

Order Additional Copies From

SAIN PUBLICATIONS
sainpublications.com/thenewyou

The Light Network
thelightnetwork.tv/thenewyou

Paperback – $9.95
Ebook – $6.95
Audiobook – $9.95

Orders of 20 or more will receive a bulk discount, $8.00 each